INTO DENOMINATIONALISM: THE ANGLICAN METAMORPHOSIS

by
William H. Swatos, Jr.

King College
Bristol, Tennessee

SOCIETY FOR THE SCIENTIFIC STUDY OF RELIGION
MONOGRAPH SERIES
NUMBER 2

This book contains some materials previously published in William H. Swatos, Jr. "Monopolism, Pluralism, Acceptance, and Rejection," *Review of Religious Research,* 16: 174-185; and William H. Swatos, Jr. "Weber or Troeltsch," *Journal for the Scientific Study of Religion,* 15: 129-144; and are used here with permission.

Printed by K & R Printers, Inc., Ellington, Connecticut

Library of Congress Catalogue Card Number: 79-53776
International Standard Book Number: 0-932566-01-4

Editor's Introduction

Whether it be viewed merely as a typological device, or as a theoretical construct, the church-sect distinction has been a controversal part of the sociological approach to religion. William H. Swatos, Jr.'s essay *Into Denominationalism* is likely to promote additional debate. He proposes yet a new conception of these types, and illustrates their utility through a comparative historical case study of Anglicanism in the United States and England. These efforts represent an attempt to connect the sociological and historical perspectives.

Through chance, this essay, like its predecessor, Richard Fenn's *Toward a Theory of Secularization,* continues a focus of the SSSR Monograph Series upon issues stemming from the classical period writers, especially Max Weber. While that continuity was not planned, it is welcome. It demonstrates the continued relevance and vitality of the issues that Weber, Durkheim, Marx, and the others addressed. For these reasons, as well as for the obvious value of this essay, we are indeed pleased to offer *Into Denominationalism* as SSSR Monograph Series, Number 2.

William M. Newman
Editor

Norwich, CT
June 19, 1979

TABLE OF CONTENTS

PREFACE

The thrust of this book is two-fold: On the one hand it seeks to address a sorely needed re-thinking and re-evaluation of the sub-area of the sociology of religion known as "church-sect theory". If such an inquiry is to have substantial impact, however, it must be firmly tied to empirical analysis. This leads to the second focus, a historical investigation of the processes of organizational change in the Church of England and its sister churches in Scotland and America during the seventeenth and eighteenth centuries. Broadly stated, the function of church-sect theory is to enable us to understand the interaction of the religious institution with the larger social system, particularly as these dynamics affect the belief and action structures of each as organizations. Specifically, here we will want to ask how it is that the most rigid of post-Reformation churches became one of the most liberal modern denominations. To a large extent this becomes a question of the transfer of the episcopate from England to America — a matter already well recognized by such studies as Carl Bridenbaugh's *Mitre and Sceptre* and Frederick Mills' *Bishops by Ballot*. It is my hope that by adopting an explicit social science model this book will extend such historical endeavors into a comparative sociology of religion.

In the first chapter I will discuss something of the tortuous journey that "church-sect" has undergone in the past seventy-five years and detail a model that attempts to provide a useable sociological framework for comparative historical analysis of the relationship between religious organizations and the larger sociocultural systems within which they operate. Chapters two through five constitute a historical case study of the development of Anglicanism from the Tudor background through the early nineteenth century — with the primary focus of attention shifting gradually from England to the United States. Although I do not propose a comprehensive history of the period, I do propose a sociological interpretation for the critical events of the time that provides a perspective into which details may continuously be integrated. The concluding chapter is both a summary of the preceding four and a theoretical extension of the model to subsequent questions.

In a desire to be relatively brief, the historical materials in the chapters of empirical analysis have been shorn of many details that are nevertheless relevant to the conclusions that are drawn about the meaning of these facts to the analysis as a whole. Much has been reduced to parenthetical citations or endnotes. I have tried as much as possible to include every source that I consulted and found applicable by a reference at some point in the text, as well as in the formal bibliography at the end of the book. This procedure is particularly necessary because the bibliographic material corresponds roughly to the "research instruments" of survey or experimental research and the data they produce. As with tables in a statistical analysis, I submit the multiplicity of citations and notes not as a bit of mere academic pedantry but as necessary part-and-parcel of the analysis itself.

ACKNOWLEDGMENTS

My doctoral dissertation completed in sociology at the University of Kentucky in 1973 forms the basis for this book. The current treatment represents a comprehensive revision of what I wrote then, however, and is intended to supercede it. I owe a continuing debt of gratitude to my director, James W. Gladden, whose encouragement of my work has never faltered. W. Robert Insko was my professor of church history in seminary and subsequently served on my dissertation committee. It was under his tutelage that my interest in this area was first sparked, and I continue to cherish his friendship. John Drysdale served on my committee while he was at Kentucky but left before the completion of the project. His teaching, nevertheless, opened new vistas on the nature and function of sociology — particularly by introducing me to the great Berger and Luckmann volume, *The Social Construction of Reality* — and led me to make the connections that underlie this project. As I have written and rewritten the materials that here appear as chapter one, I am reminded, too, of the substantial impact Dallas High's seminar on Wittgenstein had on my thinking about models and modeling in social science research.

It is difficult, if not impossible, for me to recount the ways in which numerous authors have influenced the development of my work. For the most part, my citations and bibliography provide sufficient acknowledgment of these debts; however, I want to make two exceptions. The first is David Little, whose *Religion, Order, and Law* has had a definite and considerable formative effect upon the way in which this study has proceeded. Since the completion of my degree, I have had the opportunity to come to know David and have learned even more from him as a result. The second is John R.H. Moorman, late Lord Bishop of Ripon, whose *History of the Church in England* guided me through the complexities which I have tried to explicate in the latter chapters of this book. The Episcopal Church in the United States today sorely needs a historian of his competence and clarity.

My years completing the doctorate were funded by the National Science Foundation. I also received a post-doctoral grant from the National Endowment for the Humanities to work in seventeenth-century materials at the Lilly Library of Indiana University. The final draft of this book was completed while I was a participant in an NEH summer seminar at the University of Florida under the direction of Solon Kimball.

I have benefited greatly from my association with members of the Society for the Scientific Study of Religion, several of whom have commented upon or otherwise contributed to my work. I think particularly of Richard Gorsuch, Paul Gustafson, Phil Hammond, Richard Means, Gert Mueller, Vatro Murvar, and the late Allan Eister. I could not have asked for a better editor than Bill Newman.

Through all of this my wife, Priscilla, has been a ready professional assistant in searching and solving untold bibliographic questions. Terri Nida read the final proofs and assisted in the construction of the index.

This book is dedicated to the memory of Willard A. Page, late Professor of Old Testament and Dean of the Episcopal Theological Seminary in Kentucky, whose friendship and confidence were bettered only by his sincerity and integrity, humility and good humor. *Adorate Dominum in atrio sancto eius.*

INTRODUCTION

In an article written at the close of his editorship of the *Journal for the Scientific Study of Religion,* James Dittes (1971) commented upon the strange persistence of church-sect theory as a sub-area of the sociology of religion in spite of continued, and often sharp criticism. He observed that in the first issue of the *JSSR* under his editorship (Fall, 1967), four highly respected sociologists wrote "obituaries" for church-sect theory. Yet, "though the pages of this journal during the last five years have contained several additional attacks . . . they have contained far more articles that have employed the types." Again, while several authors have proposed alternative approaches that they believe to be much better suited to the study of religious organization, these have yet to be repeatedly employed in actual analyses of empirical cases. On the other hand, despite a barrage of attacks for its many faults, church-sect theory has produced a significant and growing literature that has resulted in the systematization — albeit loose — of a prodigious quantity of empirical data and its subsequent presentation to the social scientific public. Whatever the reasons, it is a theoretical approach that has borne fruit in research and has been susceptible to modifications in light of that research. It may, indeed, be in its potential for use and the constant recasting of that use that church-sect theory finds at once both its weakness and its strength. This essay thus begins from the premise that church-sect theory is a live option in the contemporary sociological enterprise.

Any church-sect typology, however, must be incorporated into a theoretical scheme that takes cognizance of the dynamics of the larger sociocultural system within which a religious organization operates and with which it interacts. There is an abiding need for an integrated model for church-sect theory that will function in this way. Along with a critical evaluation of the shortcomings that have plagued previous church-sect endeavors, I will propose and detail a model for church-sect theory that is grounded in the broader, more general theoretical context of a society's central value system.

Here are some of the underlying assumptions, concepts, and strategies that provide the context for the development and application of such a model. That the religious institution of a society and the larger sociocultural system of that society interact is an assumption that I consider to be axiomatic. Church-sect theory has as its function the explication of this interaction. This was the essence of Max Weber's use of the terms when he introduced them into the sociological vocabulary. The dominant thread that has run through most church-sect theorizing since Weber is the general typing of religious groups on the basis of criteria centered around each group's attitude toward the "world" — the dominant sociocultural environment in which it exists. This "world ordering" of any society may in turn be placed on a heuristic continuum that has monopolism as one of its poles and pluralism as the other. Because of the nature of modern Western social history generally, we are more likely to study and seek explanations for the movement from monopolism to pluralism than the reverse — although we should not conceive of this as an irreversible process.

Again creating a heuristic continuum, we may term one pole of the religious group's possible attitude to the central value system "acceptance of the world," and the other, "rejection of the world." The result of a combination of these poles is a meaning context for the analysis of particular religious organizations and the structural changes they undergo as change takes place in the larger sociocultural matrix. There is, of course, no a priori assumption prohibiting the possibility of changes within a religious system having effects upon the larger system. Thus it is *interactions,* the dynamics of religion-social change, that lie at the heart of this study.

I also take it to be axiomatic that belief systems and action systems are positively correlated, even if this relationship requires a great deal more careful explication than is often done. This statement has as its corollary the proposition that the external form a religious organization takes reflects and/or is reflected by the religious organization's content or belief structure. For instance, if a religious organization's belief structure is positively oriented toward the central value system of the larger social system, its organizational structure will mirror this relationship (acceptance of the world) and vice versa. The same type of association ought likewise to be expected for a negative relationship between the religious organization and the larger society (rejection of the world). In other words, a religious organization accepting a monopolistic social system ought to show observable and regular differences from a rejecting one — or from one that is accepting of a pluralistic social system. Although the particular expression of these differences would be dependent upon the historical and cultural situations under consideration, once these are sufficiently comprehended generalization ought to ensue.

As an empirical illustration of the applicability of a model constructed with these propositions in mind, I will analyze the religious situations in England, Scotland, and America during the seventeenth and eighteenth centuries. The Puritan ideology will be considered as a major intervening variable. This critical period in Anglo-American religious history provides data that permit the comparison of both the same and different religious groups that were in direct contact with each other over time. It encompasses both monopolistic and pluralistic types of social systems, presents a variety of illustrative examples, and has a time perspective sufficient to permit the analysis of several groups at various points in their development. Thus the events in the two hundred or so years of the history of the Church of England and her American daughter that are investigated here ought not to be considered unique. In comparison with other religio-social interactions at other times and places, it should be possible to systematize certain patterns that might be considered generally or "universally" applicable.

Methodologically, I find Seymour Martin Lipset's comments in *The First New Nation* to be quite helpful. I particularly value his remarks on the interplay and fusion of specificity and generalization in sociological investigation. His grounding in Weber and his able defense of focusing analyses around societies' central value systems will be evident in the following chapters. I also take comfort in his extended note from T.H. Marshall on the legitimacy of the sociologist's use of secondary historical sources. There is, of course, no methodological strategy that is without faults. Lipset's remarks, along with the extensive material that he cites from the works of Karl Deutsch, do much to urge the continued viability of what Benjamin Nelson has termed comparative historical differential sociology. Such an approach is fully cognizant of the differences that pertain as one moves from one society to another. Secularization, for example, is not the same in the United States as it is in France, Great Britain, or Russia. At the same time one recognizes the cross-civilizational forces of sociocultural change that underlie these different cases. The challenge, then, is to develop general models of sufficiently wide applicability to render meaningful interpretations to seemingly disparate events.

One of the difficulties that plagues the sociologist drawing upon historical data for a sampling frame is how far to enter into historians' controversies of a non-factual nature that are nevertheless in some way related to his subject area. For the most part, I have tried to avoid bringing these sorts of materials into the empirical chapters of this book. However, two such controversies are of sufficient importance to the present project to deserve at least brief mention here.

The first of these is the debate surrounding the relationship of religion-in-America to religion-in-Europe. For many historians, American religious history stands in continuity with its European forbears; that is, the American religious scene is the "natural" outcome of currents firmly rooted in European religious history. Accordingly, American Christianity is interpreted as part of European Christendom, with all the historical baggage this necessarily entails. A less traditional approach has been adopted by some contemporary historians who argue quite persuasively that what we find in American religion is not continuity but radical divergence (thus Littell, 1962: ix-xx; also see Marty, 1969: 95-142 and Ahlstrom, 1970). These authors argue that America is a land of "Young Churches" and "New Christians" with problems and prospects quite different from their European counterparts. Though not without cultural or subcultural antecedents in the Old World, the United States is in this view more a prototype for currently developing nations (as Lipset guardedly suggests) than a realization of the aspirations of traditional Western European religion. It might even be argued that certain developments in European religious history since the American Revolution are more easily and fully explained in terms of a response to the First New Nation and its boldness in experimentation than simply as parallels to it.

The latter view has had an effect upon the development of this book. The historical analyses exhibit an interesting interplay between the new world and the old that is far from a one-way street. In terms of sociological significance, this interpretation has as its result a continued cross-cultural study rather than a study of one culture over time. This, of course, increases the value of this particular historical case-period for illustrative analytical purposes. Finally, the view of the American experience as representative of nations developing out of revolutionary origins suggests that a study such as this one, although based in the past, may have implications not only for our own times but also for the future of other social systems.

The second controversy centers around the weight to be assigned to the interaction of the religious institution with the larger social system in the fostering and shaping of the American Revolution (see Bailyn, 1967). There is also a related debate over the extent to which anti-clericalism (and/or its obverse, emphasis upon lay control) contributed to the American Revolution. For the sociologist, in this particular instance for example, the fact that people express anti-clericalism as one reason for desiring independence from England and a radically new form of government here is sufficient grounds for seeing this dimension of the religious institution interacting in the pluralizing process that brought the United States into being. Though we know that there are different meanings attached to the same words in different times and places, whether or not the revolutionaries (in the widest sense) were "truly" anti-clerical and motivated by "truly" religious ends in some almost mystical sense is not our concern. We do know that the American people expressed their desire for a New Nation in religious terms and that these terms had behavioral concomitants that made a difference in the form that religious organization was to take in American society and the role that it was subsequently to play there.

Again, the interest of the sociologist is in multifactoral interaction. The sociological perspective realizes the inherent dialetics of reality and depicts cause and effect in relative terms. The interest is not so much to determine the cause or causes of the American Revolution, but to chart the interaction of the religious institution within the pluralizing process, which had as one of its manifestations the American Revolution. In this sense we mean something much more than a war — in John Adams' words a "radical change in the principles, opinions, sentiments, and affections of the people . . . the real American Revolution" that "was effected before the war commenced." Naturally, when we take religion as the basis for analysis, our perspective is different from what it would be if we were to take economics or politics. "It is important to realize that by looking at the same problem from different theoretical perspectives, we increase knowledge about social processes" (Lipset, 1967: 400).

Chapter 1
THE POSSIBILITY OF CHURCH-SECT THEORY

The Beginnings of "Church-Sect"

Although the terms "church" and "sect" have a long heritage in the writings of church historians, the credit for their first attachment to sociological concepts belongs to Max Weber. It is likewise true that their first popularization among students of religion in the modern sense was by Weber's sometime associate Ernst Troeltsch. This division at the outset of church-sect theorizing manifests itself as the "Troeltschian Syndrome" in later works. Most subsequent treatments of the typology move rather rapidly over Weber to a consideration of Troeltsch. This approach, however, fails to deal adequately with the place of the typology in the whole of Weber's theoretical program and engenders the later criticism that church-sect theory has no relation to the rest of the sociological corpus. This, in turn, leads to a misconstrual of the ideal type as a methodological device and thereby to a reification of the original constructs.

Weber's sociology is united by one overarching thematic element: the nature, causes, and effects of *Rationalität*. This word is usually translated passively as "rationality" or "rationalism" but it is more meaningfully and accurately rendered "the process of the rationalization of action" or, I would prefer, "the rationalization-disenchantment process." The latter translation reflects an *activity* that manifests itself in secularization and secularistic pluralism. Weber was attempting to answer the question of why the rationalization-disenchantment process had come to fruition most completely in Western European society, and as such, he was a student of social change in a most fundamental sense. He was concerned with the alterations that occurred at the societal level to permit a virtually wholly secularized social structure to develop at this particular time-space juncture.

Both rationalization-disenchantment and secularization are complicated notions and difficult to explicate in a brief treatment. Clearly rationalization refers not only to the development of technical-instrumental processes based upon empirically-grounded and efficiency-directed reason *(Zweckrationalität)*, but also to a rationalization of values, in that ethical-moral thought comes likewise to be grounded in these categories *(Wertrationalität)*. Disenchantment *(Entzauberung)*, a concept arising later and much less frequently in Weber's work, refers to the progressive demystifying or "desupernaturalizing" that is a concomitant of rationalization at the systemic level (see Abramowski, 1966; Little, 1974a; Mueller, 1977). Secularization is the institutional manifestation of disenchantment. It refers not to "worldliness" in a theological or ethical sense but to the process by which the religious institution and the transcendent system of values it embodies

1

exercise less and less control over the activities of the social system as a whole. Often secularization brings with it value pluralism, particularly regarding the nature of transcendent reality, and it is this total nexus that figures into Weber's thought.

As a part of his whole project, Weber also had to develop a methodology that would permit him to resolve the dilemma of his commitment to the principle that sociology was a scientific discipline on the one hand, and on the other, of the difficulty in supplementing *verstehende Soziologie* with anything even approximating experimental accuracy.[1] How could the sociologist develop at least a "common sense" explanation of reality — one which would enable him to go on to a meaningful understanding of a concrete course of action — whether or not it were "causally adequate" in an experimental sense? Weber's answer was the comparative method, that is, the comparison of the largest possible number of cases (both historical and contemporary) relevant to the action or action-system to be explained. This, however, did not in itself solve his problems, since it was inadequate and imprecise, having no standard upon which to base its comparisons. Utilization of this method could thus easily lead to the charge that it was founded upon pure subjectivism and designed only to support the foregone conclusions of this or that researcher.

The presuppositions of "value free" science demanded a methodological tool that would at once establish a standard for comparison and provide a means whereby a variety of data could be compared. Weber answered this need with the "ideal type" *(Idealtypus),* a hypothetically concrete reality, a mental construct based upon relevant empirical components, formed and explicitly delineated by the researcher to facilitate precise comparisons. "Ideal not in the sense of the way it *ought* to look in real life but in the sense of a logically coherent and accentuated abstract construction" (M. Hill, 1973: 262). The *set* of qualities itself achieves existence only in our thought processes, but nevertheless enables us to compare external "events" to each other (see Weber, 1949: 89-112). "The ideal type, as Weber fashioned it, was designed as an operation *verstehen* — to give an understanding 'inside look' . . . and, *in this limited sense,* an 'explanation' for specific kinds of action" (Eister, 1967: 87).

The type is thus a tool in empirical analysis. "It is a conceptual construct *(Gedankenbild)* which is neither historical reality nor even the 'true' reality" (Weber, 1949: 93). It is framed in terms of the knowledge available to the researcher beginning a study and, of course, in terms of the empirical situations which one is trying to understand. These two criteria for type construction Weber termed "objective possibility" and "causal relevance" respectively. Once a researcher comes to the point at which the phenomenon under consideration is sufficiently understood or comprehended (in the sense that one can say, *Ich verstehe),* the type loses its utility and must either be modified to permit newer, more sophisticated understandings, be consigned to the realms of pedagogy as a historical residue, or be discarded. "At the very heart . . . lies not only the transciency of all ideal types *but* also at the same time the inevitability of new ones" (Weber, 1949: 104).

It was, then, in the context of his global study of *Rationalität* that Weber introduced the ideal types "church" and "sect" into the sociological vocabulary. Weber was trying to understand the processes by which Judeo-Christianity and the social systems of Western Europe and Anglo-America interacted to bring about the pluralizing and secularizing of their respective cultures (see B. Nelson, 1973). How did ascetic Protestantism and rational capitalism grow simultaneously and reciprocally into the clearly dominant position that appeared to be theirs as Weber was writing? "Church" and "sect" were introduced as two idealized types of arrangement of a single element in the organization of the religious institution, that is, the mode of membership.[2] By this dichotomous distinction, Weber was able to draw some conclusions about the movements of certain currents within Christianity that interacted with the rationalization-disenchantment process to reinforce each other.

The introduction of these two types, then, was but an incident in the attempt to understand the empirical world and to permit the sociological analysis of historical data:

> ... the ideal type is an attempt to analyze historically unique configurations or their individual components by means of genetic concepts. Let us take for instance the concepts "church" and "sect." They may be broken down purely classificatorily into complexes of characteristics whereby not only the distinction between them but also the content of the concept must constantly remain fluid. If, however, I wish to formulate the concept of "sect" genetically, e.g., with reference to certain important cultural significances which the "sectarian spirit" has had for modern culture, certain characteristics of both become *essential* because they stand in an adequate causal relationship to those influences. However, the concepts thereupon become ideal-typical in the sense that they appear in full conceptual *integrity* either not at all or only in individual instances. Here as elsewhere every concept which is not purely classificatory diverges from reality [Weber, 1949: 93-94].

The type is thus posed only as a "hypothetical individual" created for comparative purposes. Although it must be empirically related to concurrent realities, it is not a generalized abstraction, an evaluative stereotype, or a quantitative average. "It has the significance of a purely ideal *limiting* concept with which the real situation or action is *compared* and *surveyed* for the explication of its significant components" (Weber, 1949: 93). The comparison that is made is analytic, not evaluative. Whereas statements to the contrary appear regularly in today's elementary treatments of his work, Weber obviously considers the type to be something *more than* a classificatory or purely descriptive scheme. Although the methodological specifications are complex and not entirely clear in Weber's own writings (see Rogers, 1969), typology and taxonomy are not the same thing.

We can further sharpen our picture of the Weberian typology by noting what happened to the methodological qualities of this device in the transition from Weber's writings to Troeltsch's treatment in his *Social Teachings of the Christian Churches*. Troeltsch was a theologian attempting to relate types of religious experience to the varieties of social teachings with which they might be correlated.[3] In so doing, he departed from Weber on two critical points. First, he shifted the emphasis of the type from organization to behavior, a legitimate change if it better served his analytical purposes. Second, he heavily stressed the notion of "accommodation" or "compromise." The first departure is most clearly seen in Troeltsch's positing *three* types of religious behavior: churchly, sectarian, and mystical. The third of these is now simply dropped from consideration by "church-sect" theorists. Nevertheless, its presence at the outset of Troeltsch's discussion suggests that he was actually dealing with something different from that for which he is usually cited. This is particularly so given the difference between Troeltsch's combination of these elements, versus Weber's separation of organization from behavior through a church-sect distinction on the one hand, and an asceticism-mysticism dichotomy on the other (see Weber, 1973; Mueller, 1973). In any case, Troeltsch's introduction of these subsequently perceived "organizational" types was not intended to establish a standard for all further sociological investigation. The "dichotomy" of church-sect that has been attributed to Troeltsch — whatever its value — must be understood within his three-way scheme and within the instrumental context of the Weberian ideal type as well.

What was the relationship between Weber and Troeltsch with regard to this issue? Troeltsch shared with Weber primarily method, partially content, and peripherally project. In short, Weber and Troeltsch were working on different although related questions (see B. Nelson, 1975). Troeltsch understood Weber's concept of *Idealtypus,* capitalized on its "transiency," and made church, sect, and mysticism work for his own purposes.

The subsequent error of church-sect theorists has been to over-emphasize the Weber-Troeltsch association to such an extent as to assume that because Troeltsch appeared to use Weber's methodology and to some extent his content, the intention of Troeltsch's work was the same as Weber's. Ignoring the uniqueness of Troeltsch's contribution and discounting his "mystical" excesses, he has been reduced to the parrot or medium of Weber. *What Troeltsch himself calls a "sociological formulation" of a theological question has been misidentified with Weber's attempt to solve a sociological problem.* Thus many of the difficulties that have befallen church-sect theory since its original sociological use by Weber are due to an ironic failure to pay sufficient attention to *that* use in the whole structure of his sociological project. Gustafson (1967: 68) is right, for example, when he says that "typologies continue to be used with clarity only when they are used in their original frame of reference." For the social scientific study of religion that use is more properly Weber's sociology than Troeltsch's theology.

If we go back to the "rough ground" to get our bearings straight, as Wittgenstein would urge, we go back to Weber, not Troeltsch. The fact that they were colleagues with similar interests who for a while lived in the same apartment building, enjoyed one another's company, and occasionally paid their respects to one another's scholarship in their works or at scholarly gatherings, does not justify the osmosis effect the Troeltschian Syndrome forces us to infer.

We see the difference between the two men's projects clearly in the critical distinguishing elements that form the focus for each one's work. While Weber looks to "mode of membership," Troeltsch adopts "accommodation" or "compromise." Although Adams (1961) has claimed that Troeltsch was intending to use these concepts in a value-neutral way, Alan Eister (1967: 87) more properly noted their results in saying that, "By stressing the 'accommodative' character of the church (and the non-accommodative character of the sect) — and by tying these to 'compromise' (or noncompromise) of the Christian ethic, Troeltsch introduced what in effect is an open invitation, if not a demand, for subjective value-laden definitions. For what is 'compromise' of an ethic to one believer — or even to a non-believer — is *not* compromise to another." Whatever the reasons, it was Troeltsch's application of "church" and "sect" (taken out of the specific context of his theological project) that came to set the stage for virtually all approaches that were to be made within the framework during the following fifty years. Weber's methodological contribution was practically ignored.

One factor that may account for the eventual disjuncture of Troeltsch's church-sect theorizing from Weber's work on ideal types may be the order and fashion in which they were introduced to English-speaking American readers. The first major American writing to use the types was the work of another sociologically-inclined theologian, H. Richard Niebuhr in *The Social Sources of Denominationalism* (1929). Though at times possessed by a rather naïve evolutionism and narrow perspective, Niebuhr's work contributed a significant element that was lacking in earlier treatments. He used church and sect as poles of a continuum, rather than simply as discrete categories. Niebuhr did not merely classify groups in relation to their relative sect-likeness or church-likeness, but analyzed the dynamic process of religious history as groups moved along this continuum. An unfortunate result of Niebuhr's work, however, was that taken by itself it tended toward the reification of the types and the hypothetical continuum which he in turn posited. It thus contained further seeds for church-sect theory to develop (falsely) into a quasi-evaluative device:

> Here precisely is where the conceptions of "church" and "sect" as they were formulated by Max Weber can be shown to be superior for social scientific purposes to those formulated by the theologians and Christian ethicists, Troeltsch and Niebuhr; for Weber makes no reference whatsoever to whether or not *either church* or *sect* is "compromised." A *church,* for Weber, is, strictly speaking, simply a religious organization which claims monopolistic authority and into which one is born, whereas a sect is a *voluntary* religious association to which one must apply for membership and be judged worthy or not to be permitted to join (or remain) in the group [Eister, 1973: 380].

This disjunctive situation was compounded by the fact that Troeltsch's *Social Teachings* was translated in 1931, while Weber's methodological work was not available in translation until 1949. Many of the subsequent difficulties that plagued church-sect theory may be traced in part to the strange movements of this framework and its methodological base across the Atlantic.

Elaboration, Reaction, and Revision

Subsequent elaborations of church-sect theory have been clearly dependent upon the work of Troeltsch and Niebuhr. The "church-sect dichotomy" is now interpreted as a continuum having a multi-criteria basis for its analyses. Howard Becker was the first American trained as a sociologist to use and extend church-sect theory.[4] Attempting to facilitate increased specificity, Becker (1932: 624-628) delineated two types within each of the original two types, resulting in a cult-sect-denomination-ecclesia model. In thus developing the typology, Becker abandoned the Weberian device of the ideal type. Instead he moved closer, as Gustafson (1967: 65-66; see McKinney, 1966:24) has noted, to a notion of "abstract collectivities," ideal realities rather than constructs.

J. Milton Yinger in *Religion and the Struggle for Power* (1946: 18-23; see also 1957: 142-145) increased the limitations for specific points along the continuum, extending Becker's four types to six: cult, sect, established sect, class church/denomination, ecclesia, and universal church.[5] Yinger went further in his specification, however, by subtyping sects in terms of their relationship to the social order, whether they were accepting, avoiding, or aggressive. This development began a wave of interest in the "sect" type within church-sect theory, with numerous writers offering their thoughts on the best way of treating this possibility.[6] The result has been a flood of "types" based upon a variety of criteria. The impression is thus created that the task of church-sect theory is no longer to facilitate comparative analysis, but to formulate a classificatory system for the application of sociological jargon to religious organization. This is the very opposite of Weber's intention, and hardly a laudable goal in any case. Whether the blame for this should be placed on Troeltsch or his successors is a matter of some debate (see Robertson, 1970: 115; Schwartz, 1970: 56), but it is certainly accurate to say that this situation was the *result* of Troeltsch's work as it was interpreted by subsequent generations of students.

On the heels of these developments came criticism of the framework as it had come to be known in its contemporary American form. A number of critics denounced the orientation as meaningless, or at the very best woefully inadequate to any systematic investigation of the empirical world.[7] Church-sect theorizing has been criticized as ambiguous and vague, lacking precise definitions, unsuited to tests for validity and reliability, merely descriptive rather than explanatory, less informative than other possible approaches, and as unrelated to the rest of sociological theory. Despite all of these problems, many of which are more a function of the *misuse* of church-sect theory rather than inherent to it, the theoretical framework into which it has evolved has allowed a tremendous amount of data to be organized and reported (see the numerous examples cited in the excellent bibliographies in Yinger, 1970: 280-281 and Eister, 1973: 403-408). It is necessary, then, to examine the difficulties upon which the critics of church-sect typologizing base their objections, and at the same time ask whether or not these difficulties are inherent to the typology in its original Weberian context.

The most serious criticisms of church-sect theory that have been offered center upon the ideal type as a methodological device. Based on the attention given to this question earlier, it is obvious, for example, that any attempt to try to deal with the truth or falsity of an ideal type in and of itself has missed the point. The ideal type simply does not permit these sorts of considerations: "The attempts to determine the 'real' and the 'true' meaning of historical concepts always reappear and never succeed in reaching their goal" (Weber, 1949: 104-105). Except in the sense of the criterion that Weber termed "objective possibility," that an item included in the type does not violate existing scientific knowledge, the same is true of considerations of validity. Reliability is similarly limited to the relative explicitness with which the components of the typology are articulated in relationship to the use to which the typology is being put.

The typing structure has also been misused by researchers attempting to "grade" religious bodies not for comparative analytical purposes but using the type as a value-standard, thus violating the essence of Weber's "value free" comparative methodology. Others have adopted the "continuum" approach only to plot groups along the continuum as if it were a standard by which progress or regress could be measured, what Eister (1967: 85) calls "the frequent confusion of sect-to-Church 'hypothesizing' with Church-sect 'typologizing'." Any of these approaches may, of course, yield accurate theological statements or may be "valid" normative judgments from a given perspective, but none is a result of the Weberian, i.e. *sociological,* use of the ideal type.

6

Furthermore, the fact that an ideal type is a *tool* means that it can be refined generally or for a specific purpose. To say, for example, that church-sect theory is useless because it applied to pre-1800 Europe or applies only to Judeo-Christian religious groups, implies that this typing device has a supra-empirical reality. This, of course, is counter to Weber's methodology. To take a related type, for example, the concept of a "religious" person may be subjected to total and radical alteration in the attempt to map more accurately empirical events, or it may be adjusted only slightly to fit differing cultures. "Church-sect" as Weber developed it was never meant to depict eternal verities, but to provide a tool that could be altered as necessary to accomplish more adequately the particular project in which it was used. "The construction of abstract Ideal Types recommends itself not as an end but as a means" (Weber, 1949: 92).

Finally, the assertion that the ideal type methodology embodied in church-sect theory forces data into preconceived molds must be dismissed. As soon as a linguistic form is given to data, they have been molded. The question is never, "Are our data forced into a mold?" but, "Are our data so molded that they enable us to know better the world in which we live?" If the goals of science are in any sense understanding and prediction, then any tool that aids in the accomplishment of these ends (ethical matters "bracketed" for the moment) is legitimate as a methodological device, and "the value of a definition (i.e. of a concept) is only to be determined by its fruitfulness in research and theorizing" (Bottomore, 1971: 37).

In response to these criticisms, numerous scholars have made revisions within the church-sect framework, making it a more viable theoretical orientation for the sociology of religion.[8] Yinger (1970), Gustafson (1967, 1973), Roland Robertson (1970), and Wallis (1975a), for example, have each suggested the value of an explicit visual scheme for modeling and analysis. Bryan Wilson, whose work on sects has now spanned over twenty years, has come increasingly to accept a Weberian approach, though he continues to see Troeltsch as the father-figure of church-sect theory. In *Magic and the Millenium* he admits to a shift in his own thinking "from taxonomy *somewhat* in the style of ideal types to a much more thorough attempt to ideal-typification." He adds that "by using this heuristic device to measure variations from the ideal-typical and to relate them to specific empirical factors, propositions of high explanatory value might be produced . . . . This is clearly a more significant exercise in sociology than is simple classification of sects" (1973: 20).

In his seminal article "The Denomination," David Martin (1962) has forced a reconsideration of this organizational form as a type *sui generis* and required a more adequate frame for organizing reality than those we have had in the past. Martin argues that the peculiar qualities of the denomination as a type must be treated seriously and that it cannot be ignored in its historic specificity nor simply reduced to a step on a "continuum." Implicitly Martin also demonstrates that Weber's "mode of membership" criterion is inadequate for assessing all of the organizational dynamics that church-sect purports to address.

In his later pathbreaking study *Pacifism,* Martin attempts to interrelate the various types of religious organizations. At the same time he demonstrates both the applicability of his modified framework to *secular* pacifism, and the inappropriateness of treating cultism within this context. Unfortunately the book is flawed at its outset by the accrued confusions of the Troeltschian Syndrome.

"The basic categories," he writes, come "from the work of Troeltsch and Weber: the former with respect to the distinction between Church and sect and the latter with respect to his characterization of the world religions. Two analytical tasks present themselves: an expansion of Troeltsch's original [!] distinction and an attempt to see how this expansion can be combined with the work of Weber" (1966: 3). Thus, rather than seeing the problem as basically a reworking and elaboration of problems internal to Weber's work, Martin adopts the far more difficult task of pulling together two theorists whose basic interests were quite divergent.[9]

Equally significant as Martin's work is that of Benton Johnson. Early in his career, Johnson (1957) critiqued the Troeltschian approach to church-sect. In his subsequent work (1963, 1971), he returned to Weber, not to his discussion of church-sect *per se,* but to the distinction between emissary and exemplary prophets. From this perspective Johnson focuses upon the single universal variable property of a group's relationship to the social environment in which it exists. "Church" is employed as the polar type of acceptance of the social environment, while "sect" is the polar type of its rejection. This conceptualization is similar to an earlier one proposed by Peter Berger (1954), in which the more-difficult-to-operationalize variable "nearness of the spirit" was the central focus. Recently Bryan Wilson has also embraced "response to the world" as "the principle criterion of classification" of sects in an ideal-typical way (1973: 19).

Johnson contends that the sociologist should strive toward the discovery of universal properties at a high level of generality which vary in such a way that typologies might be constructed. "The major theoretical aim of sociology," he argues, "is to elucidate a variety of particular problems by means of a limited number of concepts and principles of general applicability" (1963: 542). He sees "acceptance/rejection of the social environment" as a single variable around which empirical church-sect distinctions may be grouped and asserts a certain superiority for this typological approach over that which simply adds types as historical circumstances alter.

Although Johnson's model possesses definite advantages in terms of conceptual simplicity, its lack of integration of the historical differences in the basic social structures in which the religious organizations under consideration function produces considerable difficulties that, if unchecked, could undermine the very nature of the Weberian ideal type (see Weber, 1949: 101). In short, this theoretical scheme manages to comprehend the basic property of the "internal" religion component of religio-social interaction but fails to provide adequate theoretical grounding for the integration of this property with any theory of the sociocultural system within which the religious organization may be located. For example, there is no explanation on his part of how the distinction between "church type" and "denomination type" comes to be. That he senses such a distinction and that it has something to do with the multiplication of voluntary associations in modern society is quite clear from his work (1971: 160-163). But from a theoretical standpoint *how or why* this has happened is never broached.

Monopolism, Pluralism, Acceptance, and Rejection

The purpose of this book is to present a model that contributes to church-sect theory through the inclusion of a second universal variable property that will conceptualize the orientation of a society's organization for universe-maintenance (and thus its central value system). Reference to this variable complements Johnson's work by providing a linkage between the "internal" religion component of religio-social interaction and a more general theory of social conditions external to, but interacting with, the religious organization. The model thus integrates the continuing interaction of religious organizational forms with societal-level variables. The concepts of "monopolism" and "pluralism," especially as used by Peter Berger (1969; see also Berger & Luckmann, 1967) as poles of orientation of social organization for universe-maintenance, provide the theoretical formulae for the resolution of the present problem. Berger uses these two concepts in dealing with secularization and its effects upon the shape of religion under varying circumstances, as well as its interactive effects upon the sociocultural system itself.

In a monopolistic society all facets of life are pervaded and controlled by a single system of ultimate meanings and values. In monopolistic society, there is but one religion, and it is inseparable from the socio-political power structure. Religion thus has a controlling interest over the social structure as a whole and hence a compulsive character.[10] In a situation of religio-cultural pluralism, voluntarism is the key principle for religious organization. In pluralistic society there are both competing religious groups, and competition between "religion" and other discrete institutions for the time, money, and affection of individuals and groups (see P. Berger, 1970: 42-44).

Thus religion undergoes a process of differentiation in a double sense. The first of these concerns differentiation within religious systems themselves; the second, the differentiation of the religious element from the nonreligious elements in the more general system of action. In the latter context the general developmental trend may be said to be from fusions of religious and nonreligious components in the same action structures [monopolism], to increasingly clear differentiation between multiple spheres of action [pluralism]. [Parsons, 1964: 276].

Furthermore, at the level of the individual actor in a monopolistic society there is likely to be a greater tendency toward role integration and a holistic conception of the social order. In a pluralistic society role conflicts and a fragmented or "pigeonhole" view of the sociocultural system is more likely. Theologically one would expect the god-figure(s) of the monopolistic society to be compulsive. Pluralistic god-figures would, in contrast, most likely be persuasive.

The poles of "monopolism" and "pluralism," then, function for the understanding of social organization for universe-maintenance at the level of the sociocultural system as "acceptance" and "rejection" do for church-sect theory in its more usual limited context. Joined together, the four provide an adequate theoretical context within which typologizing may proceed. These two continua thus restore the original Weberian use of "church-sect" as a tool for investigating the interacting social forces that have contributed to the rationalization-disenchantment process. In short, we return to the Weberian project but take with us the lessons of the accumulated achievements and failures of the discipline since his writing.

Given these four theoretical concepts forming the boundary-creating poles of two intersecting axes, a model may be developed in which five types are located.[11] Four of the types are based upon the quadrants of the model: Monopolism-Acceptance ("church" type), Pluralism-Acceptance ("denomination" type), Monopolism-Rejection ("entrenched sect" type), and Pluralism-Rejection ("dynamic sect" type). The fifth is a transitional anomic type located at the intersection of the continua ("established sect" type).

Although the merits of doing so could be debated, I have used terms from the traditional language of the church-sect framework to denote each of the five types. All of the types lie within the universe bounded by the polar concepts and provide a basis for comparison between groups or within a group over time. The model also permits the user to see the possibility of interactive effects between the religious variable and the larger sociocultural system. It thus accounts for societal-level variables, allows for the possibility of change in the organizational forms that a given religious group may assume, and notes the occurrence of rebounding effects from the group to the society.

On the other hand, the necessity or the rapidity of the change process is not dogmatized. No claim is made, for example, that a religious group necessarily begins as an entrenched sect and then *must* move through a series of stages ending as a church or else cease to exist. Rather, a group may initially be classified comparatively in *any* of the five types depending upon the external social conditions. For instance, in a monopolistic system a group may begin as a church and remain in that type, or as an entrenched sect and never move to another type. The model demonstrates that as the external social conditions change, certain changes in the structural-functional forms of the religious organizations in the society may be expected. This is not to deny, however, that the initiation of these systematic changes may find its impetus in the religious organization itself. The "established sect" acts as a bridge between polar types of both organizational and social systemic conditions, and the model indicates that passage through this transitional state is expected for any group moving from one quadrant to another within the property-space. But this movement itself is not a necessary one and may never be completed even if begun. It is, of course, to be expected that, during critical periods of sociocultural change, religio-social systems may manifest certain ambiguities that result in a combination of monopolistic and pluralistic tendencies. Such a combination entails the presence of certain typological anomalies that will only resolve themselves by being viewed over a greater span of time (see Little, 1969: 129).

Finally, by combining these two continua the proposed model has a potential for quantitative analysis in church-sect theory and research. While my own methodological predilections do not lead me to encourage such activity particularly, two properties varying in relation to each other (and, of course, to other properties as well) provide the essential ingredients for quantitative recipes. The construction of appropriate *measures* for these variables, of course, is quite another matter, and it will clearly be up to others to pursue it (see, for example, Welch, 1977).

The Types

With these preliminary remarks in mind, we may focus upon the types themselves. Here I will discuss the five types in a detached and relatively abstract fashion. When we turn to the analysis of the religious situation in England and America during the controversies that surrounded the quest for an American episcopate in the seventeenth and eighteenth centuries, the functioning of the types within the model itself will become increasingly clear.

FIGURE 1
THE MONOPOLISM—PLURALISM—ACCEPTANCE—REJECTION TYPOLOGY

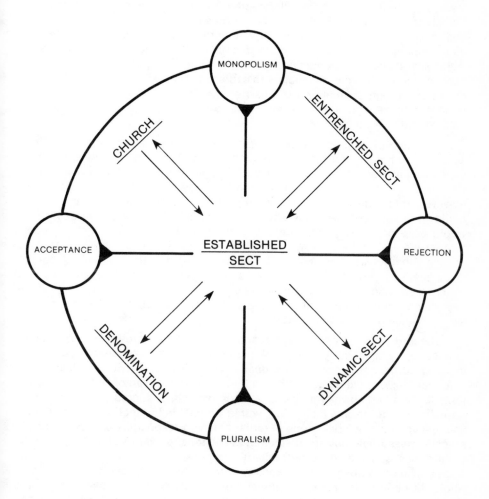

As a glance at Figure 1 will indicate, the *established sect* is at the crux of the model, and as noted earlier represents a transitional, although not necessarily short-term, stage through which any group moving from one type to another is likely to pass. It is a typological "gray area," acknowledged in some sense by the seeming contradictoriness of its name, "sect" indicating world-rejection yet "established" connoting world-acceptance.[12] I have also suggested the appropriateness of the term "anomic" in relation to this type, providing that this be understood to mean "norm confusion" rather than "absence of norms." In anomic times, furthermore, it may well be that some groups *originate* in this type.

This is the least "pure" type, almost schizophrenic in nature. It refers to that form of religious organization in which doctrine and practice on an organizational level are most likely to be disoriented by either internal or external circumstances. By internal disorientation, I mean a religious group that preaches and teaches a world-rejecting ideology as normative for its constituency and yet as an organization will accept and even emulate the values and practices of the world-view it teaches its members to reject. In contrast, external disorientation may be characterized as an inability to express to the larger society certain belief or action system changes on the part of the group that appear to be discontinuous with its past, or with the image the larger society accepts of the group in its past and present history.

In a time of prolonged anomic change some religious organizations find a semi-permanent resting place in this typological category. On the other hand, sudden changes might result in a situation in which the duration of the established sect type would be quite short. It may be stated as a general rule, however, that external systemic change (from monopolism to pluralism particularly) would produce many situations in which the established sect phase would be a prolonged one, whereas changes within the same type of social system would not be as likely to entail such long-lived established sect-like phases. Finally, in a given analysis a religious group may begin a transitional process, seem to move from one type to another, and during its established sect phase move back to where it was previously. This is particularly likely if the geographical and/or temporal context of the analysis is relatively limited, but may also occur even in a broader setting.

The *church* (Monopolism-Acceptance) is the norm for religious organization in a monopolistic society. It is a life-encompassing organizational structure that includes both corporately and individually the whole of society within its membership. For all practical purposes, it and the state are inseparably intertwined. The formalization of its own organizational structure will, of course, depend upon the formalization of the social structure within which it is to function — the relationship between the two being one of rather close correspondence. In terms of empirically measurable power, the church is the most powerful of all the organizational types considered here. Similarly, its power corresponds closely to the degree of monopolism that the society within which it functions exhibits as a whole. The church is an organizational type equally capable of being found in a "little community" as in an extensive nation-state.[13] The values of the church and the values of the "secular" society are identical, with the exactness of the identity again corresponding to the degree of monopolism in the society as a whole. In all such cases the fact of compulsion and control characteristic of monopolies is as real in religion as it is elsewhere, though it may be less obvious and formalized in the little community as compared to the larger, more complex society.

The *entrenched sect* (Monopolism-Rejection) is the church's nemesis. Its archetype is the individual dissenter within a monopolistic system, the "village atheist" of yesteryear. Depending upon the relative degree of monopolism, the entrenched sect may appear as a persecuted underground subject to criminal sanctions ranging from quite mild to capital, or a determined minority excluded legally and/or socially from the cultural and political life of the larger society. The entrenched sect does not seek equal ground with the church. It is "against the world," and either seeks to replace the present church, which it identifies with the world, or ignores the ongoing social system entirely, looking to "another world" that itself may take many different forms.

For both the entrenched sect and the church, located as they are in a monopolistic system, only external change will cause initial movement (if there is to be any) from one type to another. War, technological change, and "natural" disasters are the most frequent sources. When such change does occur, of these two groups the church will have a more difficult time in the established sect phase, adjusting its doctrine to meet the new social circumstances it faces. This is essentially a problem of downward social mobility (see P. Berger, 1969: 49). Failure to provide a plausibility structure compatible with the realities of a changed social position may eventually lead to the total disappearance of a given religious organization. The extent to which this is true will vary directly with the degree of monopolism or pluralism in the society. A monopolistic world-view has no place within it for two "churches." This is merely another way of saying that monopolism and competition are incompatible.

On the pluralistic side of the model, religious forms are more in keeping with the overarching external sociocultural perspective as well. The denomination (Pluralism-Acceptance) is for pluralism, as the church is for monopolism, the norm of religious organization (see Martin, 1962; Parsons, 1964). Bryan Wilson characterizes the denomination by saying that it is "a voluntary association" that "accepts adherents without imposition of traditional [sectarian] prerequisites of entry . . . . Breadth and tolerance are emphasized . . . . Its self-conception is unclear and its doctrinal position unstressed . . . . One movement among many . . . it accepts the standards and values of the prevailing culture . . . . Individual commitment is not very intense; the denomination accepts the values of the secular society and the state" (1959: 4-5). Save for the semantic confusion it would create, one could almost say that denominationalism is the "church" of pluralism, but with a critical difference. The emphasis in monopolism is upon the integration of sacred and secular ("church" and "state") into a single meaningful whole. Sectarians are persecuted in monopolism not only because of bigotry itself, but also because of a fear that the whole sociocultural fabric will be torn apart. In pluralism this intimacy, except perhaps as there is such a thing as "civil religion," is lost. One may belong to any denomination — *or none!* Religion is pigeonholed and privatized. It is a voluntary activity to be undertaken or dismissed at the discretion of the individual. The denomination, then, is marked perhaps most significantly by this voluntarism of support coupled to mutual respect and forbearance of all other competing religious groups. It is, indeed, this quality of *competition* that is the unique hallmark of the pluralistic religious situation (see P. Berger, 1969: 137-139), and that distinguishes it from the compulsion inherent in monopolistic control. Acceptance of the "free market" situation in religious ideas is the critical operating principle of denominationalism.

The *dynamic sect* (Pluralism-Rejection) is "dynamic" in its claim to have "the answer" in simple readily-communicable terms. Open to all but espousing high standards, it is a faith "on the move." In a different sense from the denomination, it is the "church" of pluralism. Its claims sound churchly. All are to be included, but it is not to be a church. It sets itself against the central value system of the dominant culture in a way that is explicitly defined and articulated. Although it may come to the culture and appear to participate in certain of its social systems, it does so only in an emissary way. Worldly politics in itself is rejected. It is thus the non-sectarian, non-denominational true "church" for its (or all) time. Like the denomination, it is the child of pluralism, however, because only in a pluralistic social system would it be allowed to make and pursue its claims freely. "The reaffirmation of orthodox objectivities in the secularizing-pluralizing situation, then, entails the maintenance of *sectarian* forms of socio-religious organization" (P. Berger, 1969: 164). These very claims, however, make the dynamic sect as a typological entity subject to a short life-span in any given case. One, two, or perhaps three generations are all that any group will spend here before it either moves to an established sect, into denominationalism, or for all practical purposes, out of existence.[14] In a sense, then, the dynamic sect is closest to the sect-type organization envisioned by Niebuhr.

By way of both conclusion and prolegomenon, a few things bear repeating. First and foremost is simply the reassertion that what we have been looking at and will be using are analytical *types*, not exhaustive catalogue entries. The model is analytical rather than empirical.[15] This is typology, not taxonomy. Therefore not every religious group that has ever existed in every society will be amenable to cataloguing by this scheme. The nomenclature employed is at least in one sense entirely arbitrary. What is important is not what we call a type but the meaning assigned to it. The meaning comes from the bipolar concepts and the model that has been created from them. This typology is successful to the extent that it permits users to understand the relationship between religious organization, social structure, beliefs and values in a wide variety of situations better than they would without it or with another typology. There will, no doubt, be specific groups here and there that will be difficult to analyze in terms of this typology. Whether or not this leads to its abandonment will depend upon the frequency of such incidents and the relative importance of the groups involved to the research project at hand.

Second, this approach does not prohibit sub-typing or even the construction of taxonomies. Rather, it enhances this activity. Distinguishing between sectarian forms based upon the monopolism-pluralism-acceptance-rejection typology, for example, ought to make taxonomic descriptions more fruitful theoretically, and hence, ought to give a better order to empirical descriptions. The earlier work of Bryan Wilson (1959), as well as recent developments by Michael Welch (1977), for example, ought to be thus more meaningfully integrated into a comprehensive yet simple theoretical structure.

Third, although I have said that terminology is not particularly important, I would argue that what is meant by concepts like "cult" and "order" belong to a different sphere of analysis. Both are more appropriately attached to the asceticism-mysticism dimension than to church-sect. The integration of these two areas is a matter of considerable importance, though well beyond the scope of the present endeavor. Suffice it to reaffirm here that the focus of church-sect is the relationship of the *structures* of religious expression to the larger sociocultural system and vice versa. Asceticism-mysticism primarily addresses the relationship of the *believer* to the world. This is expressed in the conjoint ideas of inner-worldly and other-worldly asceticism and mysticism. When these forms of behavior themselves come to be socially structured, such types as cult and order are useful. Since the religious structure is obviously involved at both levels, there will, of course, be some overlap.

Finally, there is the matter of what might be called "statics and dynamics." Except in the limited case of the dynamic sect, the model does not postulate necessary processes. When processes occur, they are likely to do so in specifiable ways, through which certain regularities may be observed and upon which generalizations and predictions may be based. The model also demands no beginning or end points. A denomination does not have to "grow" to that status, nor does a church necessarily "fall" from its place. Only actual changes in the society's organization for universe-maintenance or in the organization's self-concept (and/or both) are determinative. No grand scheme for all of history is here intended. The model is as "valid" for a cyclical view of history as for a linear one. Secularization may be continuous or discontinuous, and the model will work just as well.

The Anglican Possibility

Church-sect theory has been used in the past for historical studies of numerous groups that have developed in relation to the Anglican tradition. Work by Brewer (1952) and Chamberlayne (1964) on Methodism, Isichei's essay on the Quakers (1964), and Eister's on the more recent Oxford Group movement (1949), are some of the best-known examples. But there have been virtually no comparative historical treatments of the parent body. Yet Anglicanism presents a particularly well-suited case for testing the usefulness of the proposed model. Perhaps because history tends to be written from the viewpoint of the "winners" of a particular conflict, most writers have been more inclined to trace the tangible results of the rise of Puritanism than to consider the course of Anglicanism thereafter. The story of Anglicanism in England, Scotland, and America from 1550 to 1850 is a saga of tremendous social, political, economic, and cultural change. It carries with it changes in the religious institution as well.

In asking how the most rigid of post-Reformation church structures turned into one of the most liberal modern denominations, we are asking a church-sect question. The "denominationalizing" of the Episcopal Church in the United States involves process analysis rather than mere labeling. We know that it took far more for this to happen than Church of England communicants waking up one morning to discover that Cornwallis had surrendered and subsequently going to the local church to mark out "Church of England" and insert "Protestant Episcopal." Indeed, the very name "Protestant Episcopal" was some years in the making (see Shoemaker, 1959: 101-124). It is one of the many marks of conciliation that was required to unite diverse groups of American Anglicans into a workable denominational structure that would equally reflect the tradition of the Mother Church and the adjustments to a radically altered sociocultural situation in this First New Nation. Another is the development of a "primitive episcopate," so central to Mills' *Bishops by Ballot,* and to this book as well.

There is a fine line that separates social history from historical sociology. In the pages that follow I will attempt to demonstrate that the proposed model orders data in a way that provides explanatory power leading to the understanding of the complex events involved in this socio-historical process. To this end I will make reference to a number of dramatic moments or peak events that seem to mark critical changes in the religio-social structures. Nevertheless, in their fundamental character such changes should be understood as an oozing and seeping process, with much backing and filling. The sharp dramatic events and cleavages are thus a fulfillment of processes long at work in many forms. The function of the model is to capture those critical moments when things seem to come to a head and say: Here it has happened, and not by accident.

Chapter 2
MONOPOLISM AND THE ENGLISH CHURCH

The Tudor Background

The courtship preceding the monopolistic marriage of the English crown and its ecclesiastical handmaid was a lengthy and not always blissful one. A consumation was finally achieved in the promulgation by Henry VIII and his Parliament of the decrees separating the Church of England from that of Rome, and declaring Henry and future monarchs to be the Supreme Head of the Church throughout the realms they governed. A cardinal principle of Henry and of Thomas Cranmer, his Archbishop and co-reformer, was the *oneness* of England and her Church. As Herman Israel writes: "Henry VIII siezed the English branch of the Roman Catholic Church and, in effect, made it an arm of the state . . . . establishing a state monopoly over religion to enhance royal control over public life in England" (1966: 596, 598). It is clear from Henry's own statements that he never questioned the inherent catholicity of the Church of England. He never doubted that the English Church held in all *essentials* the identical faith as the Church of Rome. Earlier in his career Henry had been named "Defender of the Faith" by Leo X for an anti-Lutheran publication he was supposed to have authored. This was a title the monarch never abandoned. Norman Cantor (1967: 306) considers the spiritual link between Henry and Rome to have been so strong that he claims, "Henry VIII was no more Protestant than the Pope."[1]

What Henry insisted upon, however, was the implementation and legitimation of his conviction (heightened, no doubt, by his severe difficulties with the papacy in obtaining annulment of his marriage to Catherine of Aragon) that there was for every nation-state one Church, and *it* was the Catholic Church in and of that nation. The church and the nation were inseparable. The intervention of the Bishop of Rome in the affairs of the Church of England marked the domination of a foreign power over the nation of England. The "one nation, one church" principle Henry adopted in his break with Rome is a succinct statement of the ideal type of "church" as the model proposed here conceives it. All men of the nation are members of the church *because* they are members of the state. There can be no such thing as two churches in one nation, because there can be no such thing as a division between the powers temporal and the powers spiritual. Henry was Supreme Head of the Church as well as King of England. A royal monopoly had been staked out. As F.M. Powicke (1941: 1) states in *The Reformation in England,* "The one definite thing which can be said about the Reformation in England is that it was an act of the State."[2] Archbishop Cranmer adopted, agreed with, and adhered to Henry's policy (see Hillerbrand, 1964: 327-329; Hutchinson, 1962: 25-63; Pennington, 1954: 25-45). While there may be some doubt of his sincerity and ultimate convictions in this regard, there is little question that Cranmer followed this guiding principle as long as Henry was alive. As Archbishop he wrote in the introduction of the first *Book of Common Prayer* (1549). "Now from henceforth, all the realm shall have but one use." It was, indeed, a monopolistic era. "Nowhere was the king more emphatically the savior of society than in England" (Pollard, 1966: 25).[3]

The Henrican arrangement of church and state had long-term consequences for Anglo-American religious history. As David Little (1969: 15-22) argues, the authority structure underlying the Tudor monarchy that Henry tried to bring to maturity was *patrimonial* in character, a "type" that Weber (1947: 346-358) employs as a rather unstable subtype of traditional authority. Weber devotes much of his treatment of authority types to puzzling over the problem of the routinization of charisma, and his introduction of patrimonialism must be understood in this connection. It is the vesting of traditionally-based authority in a single figure who appears *by means of* that tradition "charismatic." In this case, that figure is the English monarch. It would take us too far off course to trace the particular conditions that gave rise to this authority structure at this juncture in English history (see Lindsay, 1962). Nevertheless, it has a direct bearing upon the continuing Erastian erosion of the Church of England, the gradual but steady denigration of the religious content (i.e. theology) of the Church until it became but an outward form for the exercise of state functions at the bidding of civil officers. The latter eventually might not even themselves claim any relationship other than a statutory one to the Church (see B.L. Manning, 1967; Dickens, 1964; Lamont, 1969). While this condition becomes demonstrably evident after the Glorious Revolution, one might trace its first "trickle" back to Henry's parliamentary maneuverings, in which his chief minister Thomas Cromwell played so large a part. The effect of these was the subjugation of ecclesiastical matters to the decision (and frequently the whim) of civil authority and secular economic interests.[4]

The difficulty that besets patrimonialism here is that it vests tremendous authority in the monarch, giving him a virtual monopoly over all that transpires in his realm. Yet at the same time, it binds him in every action to be consistent with an unwritten and frequently ephemeral supramundane "tradition" upheld by common consent in the nation over which he governs.[5] In short, it assumes that the monarch ordained of God will always exercise his power as the servant of the nation, which is always best served by loyalty to its (godly) traditions. Divine Right is thus the creation and servant of Holy Tradition. The tradition itself, however, stands over and above the power of the monarch, although according to the strictest interpretation the monarch remains accountable only to God. The tension is obvious. Given the non-static nature of social processes and the idiosyncrasies from monarch to monarch, the question in time arises: If God can exercise his will through one earthly creature, can He not also exercise it through the common consent of the many in the name of the tradition which is theirs as well as their leader's? Cranmer defended the position that even his own archepiscopal commission was derived from Henry's spiritual majesty as the Holy Ghost's proper overseer of the faithful, and that the King could legitimately ordain men to the priesthood if he so desired (see Macaulay, 1967: I 44). However, Calvin argued that the English "were guilty of blasphemy" when they called the monarch "the chief Head of the Church under Christ" (see Little, 1969: 83).

FIGURE 2
CHRONOLOGICAL CHART OF CRITICAL INCIDENTS
IN ANGLICAN RELIGIO-SOCIAL HISTORY
1535-1675

ENGLAND	NEW ENGLAND	VIRGINIA
Church of England church-like from reign of Henry VIII until 1640.		Anglicanism (of "congregational" sort) fully established when Virginia became royal colony, 1627. Remains thus throughout this period; i.e. church-like.
1640—Imprisonment of Wm. Laud, Archbp. of Canterbury. Anglicanism established sect.	"Congregational Way" church of New England. Given formal articulation in Cambridge Platform, 1648.	
1644—Abolition of episcopacy. 1645—Execution of Laud. 1649—Execution of Charles I. Anglicanism (as "prelacy") entrenched sect.	No permanent Episcopal congregations until end of 17th century. Episcopalians entrenched sect.	
1661—Restoration of Stuart line and gradual enactment of Clarendon Code. Anglicanism established sect.		

According to Weber the practical result of this tension is the replacement of patrimonialism by an authority structure of the rational-legal type. Although our interest here is not authority types but rather types of religious organization, the interaction of these two elements over time leads to differences in both that are consistent with each other. Henry created a patrimonial social system by creating a patrimonial church. Later churchmen would find that doing away with the civil *pater* might have significant ramifications upon the ecclesiastical *mater* as well.

The first difficulties of patrimonialism as the basis for an enduring plausibility structure for the English monopoly came in the successive reigns of Edward VI and Mary Tudor following their father's death. Both monarchs were much more partisan to continental theological and political viewpoints than was Henry. Young Edward followed the Protestant reformers to the extent that he allowed the Church to be divested of many of the teachings and practices Henry had considered essential to the preservation of the historic Christian faith (see Knappen, 1970: 72-102). Mary then reverted to the Roman Church, enforcing her will with a tyranny and brutality that earned her the title "Bloody Mary." Indeed, the self-imposed exile of many of the Puritans to the continent during Mary's reign was an important formative influence upon the further development of English religion.[6] But in each of these cases the essential principle of the oneness of church and state was maintained. Even Mary found that to restore the Church of England to the government of the Church of Rome, she had to accept the principle, if not the title, that she was the supreme head of the English Church. Only by this means could she once more turn the control of the church over to the Roman hierarchy. The monopoly and its church remained, but the weaknesses of the foundation for both were showing (see Moorman, 1963: 180-198; Parker, 1966: 111-141).

The Elizabethan Settlement

With the ascent of Elizabeth I in 1558, the plan and policy of the Henrican reformation found a champion that would bring its fullest realization. Not herself a zealot in religion, devoted and yet practical, capable of acting as a regal moderator between warring factions, Elizabeth was a careful monarch who realized the importance of settling the religious differences that had plagued every aspect of her nation's life since her father's death. There were by this time three recognizable parties in the Church of England: the Papists (Recusants), the Anglicans, and the Puritans.[7] Each agreed with the monopolistic "one state-one church" policy, and each felt that it alone possessed the formula by which such a policy could rightly be put into operation. Only a small group of independently-minded dissenters at the far left of the Puritan wing gave any serious thought to the possibility of an ecclesio-political structure in which something like pluralistic denominationalism could occur. These, of course, were the Separatists, ancestors of the Pilgrims, whose activities were most vigorously suppressed by Her Majesty's government (see Coolidge, 1970: 55-76; Selbie, 1912: 7-30; Wakeman, 1887: 47-49).[8]

Elizabeth's method of resolving the general party strife consisted formally of: an Act of Supremacy that revived Henry's patrimonial legislation against Rome and all that it entailed; an Act of Uniformity that reintroduced the Prayer Book with severe penalties for disobedience to its required use, but without the most objectionable insertions of the Edwardian Calvinists; and a set of Royal Injunctions modeled after those of Edward, but encouraging a more Catholic style of devotional practice. While Elizabeth was determined to preserve the English monopolistic system by enforcing uniformity, she also understood that this could be done only if both sides could find a measure of satisfaction.[9] In terms of the model, here is a thoroughgoing monopolism, with the Church of England a clearly church-like religious organization supported by and supportive of the political establishment. Elizabeth's policy of religious *toleration* was never a policy of religious *liberty*. Her goal was always comprehension in *one* church (see Jordan, 1965).

The Elizabethan Settlement made its way rapidly into the life of the English people. Apparently the divisions that occurred under Edward and Mary caused sufficient conflict to convince the people of a need for national unity, and a united church that could provide an inclusive, meaningful plausibility structure for daily life. By her general policy of religious toleration, which lasted throughout almost her entire reign,[10] Elizabeth became a cultivatedly charismatic monarch the people could accept. If the success of her scheme had not been so intimately tied to her own personality, rather than to the tradition she was supposed to embody, England might have had a state church free from outside interference or inner turmoil from then on.[11] As Moorman states, "Elizabeth distrusted the papists because of their allegiance to Rome, and the protestants because of their allegiance to Geneva. People who took their orders from some continental power were not wholeheartedly English. And that was what Elizabeth wanted — an *English* church designed to meet the spiritual needs of the English people" (1963:212). According to Little, this attitude was not merely Elizabeth's caprice. English insularity gave widespread support even among the ecclesiastics for the enshrining of "what they understood to be their hallowed institutions and traditions" (1969: 133).[12] Bernard Lord Manning (1967: 98) quips that "Anglicanism is so thoroughly English as to be extremely tiresome to describe."

The Elizabethan ideal was never fully realized. Yet without a doubt, the people as a whole were more united during this period than they had been under Elizabeth's immediate predecessors, or than they were to be for at least the next hundred years. "Church and State were two aspects of one society in Elizabethan England" (Herklots, 1966: 6).[13] Except where questions of *treason* were involved, Calvinists and Romanists alike were as much as possible accommodated in as broadly comprehensive a scheme as there was ever to be in the pre-Victorian Established Church. Everything, as the Tractarians were later to prove, was written in the most inclusive fashion possible. Thus Jordan writes that, "The Elizabethan settlement of religion was pragmatic, comprehensive, and above all else, Erastian. Dominated by a lay intelligence which measured every trend in national life in strict relation to the ends of political unity and the reign of law, the whole weight of ecclesiastical policy was employed to restrain enthusiasm, to moderate the intemperance of zealots whose aspirations might rend the nation, and to destroy those elements in the religious life of the nation which ventured beyond carefully and strictly defined bounds of treason" (1942: 67).[14]

Elizabeth thus maintained and enlivened the English Church by the fullest exercise of her personal powers in solidifying the royal monopoly. She recognized (as the model holds) that the maintenance of the monopolistic system depends upon a church-like religious organization that unites behind the monarchy. Yet, she could do no more than patch the cracks in the structure that had already become visible in the reigns before hers. She ardently appealed to the tradition of the realm in an attempt to give greater credibility to the "fiction of continuity" she was trying to write on the hearts of her people (see Little, 1969: 135). But the doctrinal vacuousness of the Settlement's plausibility structure was beginning to take its toll (see Alford, 1963: 50-51). "Under Elizabeth," Plummer remarks, "despotism was exercised, not so much in settling problems, as in refusing to have them settled" (1904: 44).

One of Elizabeth's chosen Archbishops, John Whitgift, pronounced most aptly on the state of the church when he defended his assertion that the monarch reigns supreme "in deciding matters of religion, even in the chief and principal points," by stating that, "If it had pleased Her Majesty, with the wisdom of the realm [a sense of common tradition], to have used no bishops at all, we could not have complained justly of any defect in our church." David Little observes that "Whitgift regarded as 'absurd' the Puritan notion that the basis for Church order was to be found in the Word of God — that is, in a special Word demanding special obedience. In relation to the crown's command, the Word of God is not special. To make such a claim was the central flaw in the Puritan position. Scripture, according to Whitgift, simply does not supply a system of Church order, or any other kind of order. That is not its function. If it has a function with respect to behavior, it refers man to the magistrate as the source of order" (1969: 140).[15]

The element of dogmatic content itself had become grounded for its assurance not on any numinous referent, but on the perseverance of the royal monopoly. As Perry Miller (1970: 10) notes, "When a petition from the Continent asked indulgence for advocates of more extreme reformation she [Elizabeth] replied in words that epitomize the whole situation: 'It was not with her safety, honour, and credit to permit diversity of opinions in a kingdom where none but she and her council governed'." The validity of the diverse "opinions" as theological statements never enters into consideration. The question is entirely one of monopolism or pluralism: whether, in terms of the model, England would have a church-like religious organization or move toward pluralistic denominationalism. Elizabeth and her ecclesiastics mustered all of their argumentative ammunition to assert the prerogative of her monopoly. Thus, "We hear much of the King's Majesty and the Queen's Majesty; *Thus saith the Lord* sounds rather faintly in the Tudor settlements" (B.L. Manning, 1967: 106). Few divines of the Elizabethan hegemony sensed the serious dangers that awaited Mother Church when the "national mother" would pass from their midst.[16]

Monopoly, Monarchy, and the Early Stuarts

Though the sobering experiences of the days of Bloody Mary had disposed all parties to accept the Elizabethan Settlement as a measure of peace for the time, there remained the ineluctable conflict between liberty and authority, independency and uniformity. During the following century this conflict was cast in the mold of a struggle for domination between Genevan and English ideas of the Church. The Calvinistic system of belief and worship had swept the field in Scotland and Scottish Presbyterian influence fed the fires of discontent in the sister nation [Parsons & Jones, 1937: 38-39].

The struggle that took place in pre-Revolutionary England between the Presbyterians and the Episcopalians began not as a move toward denominationalism, nor as an overt move to unseat the monarch, but as a conflict over what *the* Church of England was to be like.[17] As yet no thought was formally entertained by either of these two major politico-ecclesiastical factions that there could be two Christian bodies in one nation (see Miller, 1970: 3-52). With the succession of James VI of Scotland to become James I of England (thus joining the two states), the English Puritans' leaders felt that they might now have a chance to bring the Church into their sphere of theological influence.[18] Certainly a rather natural concomitant of the strong Jacobean attachment to the doctrine of the Divine Right of Kings was an inherent distrust of the papacy. The Presbyterians hoped that as a stranger in a country in which his immediate predecessor on the throne had put his mother (a Roman Catholic, however) to death, James would be willing to lend a sympathetic ear to their reforming schemes (see Usher, 1910). The new King called a conference in 1604 at Hampton Court over which he presided. The Presbyterians presented a petition listing the grievances they believed had been inflicted upon them by the Church of England hierarchy. Expecting triumph, they received defeat. James proved himself a keen amateur theologian not disposed to Calvinism and disappointed his fellow countrymen by zealously embracing the English form of church government, which in turn supported his theory of the monarchy. As Moorman (1963: 222) observes, "The King rules by Divine Right, and it was the duty of the Church to support him as he would support the Church. 'No Bishop, no King,' cried James at the Hampton Court Conference; but as the country was one day to learn, the saying had also its corollary: 'No King, no Bishop'."

The decision at Hampton Court was more than a determination of the nature of ecclesiastical polity and liturgical formularies. It was a rejection of the Puritan ideology that found its ecclesiastical expression in Presbyterianism, but also had far broader implications. According to James, "A Scottish Presbytery as well agreeth with a monarchy as God and the Devil." In his *Basilikon Doron,* a book of directions on government addressed to his son Prince Henry (who never came to the throne), James calls the Puritans "very pests in the Church and commonweal," adding, "I protest before the great God that ye shall never find with any Highland or border thieves greater ingratitude and more lies, and vile perjuries, than with these fanatic spirits." Elsewhere he recalls, "I was calumnated in their sermons not for any vice in me but because I was a king, which they thought the highest evil." James may have perceived the latent pluralizing and secularizing tendencies of Puritanism much more acutely than did many of his fellow royalists or their successors.[19]

In the Jacobean 1604 *Canons* the first clause of the canon defining a true member of the Anglican Church states that he is "One who confesses that the King's supremacy over the Church in causes ecclesiastical is legitimate" (see Hart, 1968: 27-28). James so identified the Anglican religious hierarchy and the monarchy as to create a web of monopolistic privilege that would eventuate in the relative powerlessness of both. At a time when James and the Puritans might have found a theological meeting ground in a "purely spiritual" or "primitive" episcopacy, i.e. one that had no civil function, he instead used the ecclesiastical machinery of the church to bolster his self-serving devotion to a strict ideal of "Divine Right," a conception challenged in the courts of law (see W. Jones, 1971) and finally defeated by the New Model Army during the reign of his successor (see Plummer, 1904: 54-61). James had so intertwined the courts, the church, and the royal monopoly as mutually legitimating plausibility structures that orderly redress of grievances became increasingly impossible. Perhaps fearing a warning by Elizabeth, "There is risen a sect of perilous consequences who would have no kings but a presbytery" (in Gooch, 1954: 36), James told the bishops, "If once you were out and they in place, I know what would become of my supremacy" (in Hart, 1968: 27).

James' rule differed from Elizabeth's, however, because he refused to accept the patrimonialism of the monarch's rule *sub deo et lege.* For him *sub deo* was sufficient (see Little, 1969: 186-189). As the Anointed of God ruling by Divine Right, James demanded absolute obedience from his subjects, obedience for which he found strong arguments in Elizabethan ecclesiology. What James apparently failed to sense throughout his reign, however, was that it was because Elizabeth was a ruler who exercised her power under God *and law* that the theologians so espoused the cause of the monarchy.[20] Because of the Elizabethan dedication to and assumption of the principle of King-in-Parliament, the Anglican divine in her reign could give ecclesiastical sanction to a principle of absolute obedience to the monarch. As the first estate of Parliament, the Lords Spiritual had a sufficient wedge to protect their interest. They could exalt the monarchy to the heights by assuming themselves to be included in that institution (see Mason 1913: 23-166).

James, on the other hand, declared it treason to affirm that the king should be under law, adopting a King-above-Parliament stance. This placed the theologians in an embarassing position. They chose to defend the monarchy, rather than move toward a "disorderly" refinement of dogma (see Lamont, 1969: 28-77). This should not surprise us. The monarchy, as James exercised its privileges, was the safest bulwark against a wholesale liquidation of both the financial and spiritual structure that supported the English Church against its Puritan "reformers." If it had been implemented, the clerical scheme the Puritans proposed would have had severe repercussions upon the ecclesiastical economics of the time.[21] An alliance between the clergy and the monarchy was forged not only on spiritual and political grounds, but on economic ones as well. It carried over into the reign of Charles I and caused the Puritan sympathizer Thomas Fuller to write of the establishment divines, "In all state alterations be they never so bad, the pulpit will be of the same wood with the Council-board" (in Gooch, 1964: 54). Thus by the conclusion of James' reign the monopolistic system was pushing ever more strongly toward the polar extreme, carrying with it and being carried by the church-like religious structure. At the same time, there was a growing opposition to this polar monopolism, an opposition that eventually exploded into full revolt (see Mitchell, 1957; Tolmie, 1977; Watts, 1978).

When their reigns are superficially compared, James and Charles Stuart seem to be but two products of the same mold. Both tried to enforce episcopacy in an unwilling northern kingdom, both despised the Puritans, both insisted on reigning *sub deo solo,* and both so meshed episcopacy into their political philosophy and praxis that king, bishop, and monopolistic privilege each came to imply the other two. In spite of these similarities, there was at least one important difference in the two men. While James had personal aggrandizement as his goal, Charles was pursuing the realization of an ideal.[22] Whatever value we may place on these differing ends, the result of Charles' policy was the more onerous. Though James could be mellowed by money or favors, Charles pursued his "Thorough" course with idealistic singlemindedness. Bolstered by his lieutenants, the Earl of Strafford and the Archbishop of Canterbury, Charles set out to purge the nation of every ounce of Puritan sentiment. "In the sixteenth and seventeenth centuries the Church had a monopoly of thought-control and opinion forming . . . sermons were for the majority of Englishmen their main source of political information and political ideas. Control of the pulpit was a question of political power" (C. Hill, 1967: 36, 38). Charles thus insisted that his priests be preachers of obedience to the monarchy or be silenced. Sir John Coke, Secretary of State from 1625 to 1939, an ardent Royalist (not to be confused with Edward Coke), maintained that the primary function of the clergy "is now the defence of our CHURCH, and the rein of our STATE" (in C. Hill, 1964: 127).

As Figgis (1922: 282) rightly notes, the doctrine of Divine Right, as the Stuarts practiced it, was an "assertion of the civil as against the ecclesiastical authority." Such a system needed a strong plausibility structure that would allow the monarch great latitude, while keeping him free from criticism by his subjects. James maintained that "Kings are not only God's lieutenants here below and sit upon God's thrones, but even by God Himself are called gods [in Psalm 82]" (in Moorman, 1963: 226). So Charles' Archbishop William Laud asserted, "The King's power is God's glory; and the honour of the subject is obedience to both" (in Miller, 1970: 12). Laudian Anglicanism provided the necessary legitimating scheme for the continuation of the Stuart doctrine, at the same time reaping the harvest as the Puritan tares were cast out of office in church and state. "To accuse Laud and his bishops of interfering in social and political affairs is ridiculous," comments Trevor-Roper (1962: 5), "for social and political affairs were their business" (see also C. Hill, 1956: 320 ff., 1967: 354-381). Despite the fact that Laud felt he was akin to the earlier reformers and that his vision of a national church was consonant with their dreams, the people could not tolerate his interference in local affairs and the oppression that resulted from his high-handed tactics. Laud did not use his power lightly or irresponsibly. Though not above corporal punishment, he disliked it, and never put anyone to death. "He was able, and, like so many in his age, he was wholly convinced that he was right" (Herklots, 1966: 29). Laud's own words explain his motives: "Ever since I came in place, I laboured nothing more than that the external worship of God, too much slighted in most parts of this kingdom, might be preserved, and that with as much decency and uniformity as might be; being still of the opinion that unity cannot long continue in the Church where uniformity is shut out at the church door" (also see Addison, 1952; Searle, 1969).

The Puritan party thus entered into a new phase in its development. Ejected quickly and often cruelly from participation in civil and church life as they had never been before, the Puritans were faced with several unattractive choices. They could, of course, conform to the Laudian project, decry their slippage from the "faith once delivered to the saints," and continue to participate in English society. In terms of the model, they would do what was necessary to remain a part of the church in a monopolistic society. On the other hand, they could choose to go "underground," continue to assert the rightness of their position and suffer the consequences. At their mildest, this would mean meeting in secret and in constant fear of informants. At their worst, mutilation or even death. Collinson (1967: 465-466; see also Watts, 1978) suggests that as the Stuarts forced Puritanism underground, the multiplication of sects that became a Puritan hallmark was initiated. Obviously this is an approximation of the church's nemesis, the entrenched sect. But unlike most church versus entrenched sect situations, the Puritans had another alternative that would allow them (for the time being) to retain their English citizenship and tongue, and also give them freedom to follow their consciences in religious matters. They could go to America, a New World.

The Monopoly Extended and Tested

By the prerogative of the royal monopoly, two companies were formed in the early years of the seventeenth century to colonize the "countreys lying North of Florida" which the English believed Providence had entrusted to them. It was James' policy to grant patents for colonization to his court favorites or those who could persuade him that it would benefit him financially (see Little, 1969: 215-216; Rowse, 1965: 206-237). One grant was that of the "First Colony," which after 1609 became known by its more familiar title, the Virginia Company. The other, the Plymouth Company, was to colonize the northern parts of the vast new continent. The first settlers of the Plymouth group arrived at Monhegan Island in 1607. Their chaplain conducted services according to the *Book of Common Prayer*. The King had given both companies of early colonists certain "divers Articles, Instructions, and Orders" that stated, in part, "That the said Presidents, Councils, and the Ministers [of the colonies], should provide, that the true Word and Service of God be preached, planted, and used, not only in the said Colonies, but also, as much as might be, among the Savages bordering upon them, according to the Rites and Doctrine of the Church of England" (see Stith, 1865: 37). As Raymond W. Albright (1964: 15) observes in his history of the American Episcopal Church, "Had this colony been permanent it might have made a vast difference in the history [and sociology] of New England and perhaps of the entire nation . . . . It remains quite clear, then, that long before Pilgrims or Puritans arrived in Massachusetts, the Church of England was by charter established in that colony and its worship regularly practiced."[23]

That this colony did virtually cease, that the Puritans and Pilgrims did land in and gain control over the inhabited New England regions, and that the members of the Church of England remaining loyal to the episcopate were forced for some time there into an entrenched sect-like position against the Congregational establishment, are in great measure the factors responsible for the eventual differences between the northern and southern church life of Episcopalians. The entrenched sect-like position of the Anglicans in New England compared to the church-like Anglican religious organization in the South had significant consequences for the American Episcopal Church as the pluralizing processes of American society moved toward denominationalism.[24]

The First Shall be Last

Until the revocation of the Virginia Company charter by the King and Privy Council in 1624, making Virginia a royal colony and Anglicanism the official "state church," the leadership in all spheres, including religion, was entirely in the hands of the Company. The latter, of course, were expected to comply with the Royal Injunctions given on a variety of subjects, including church life and worship. The Prayer Book was used, and services were conducted wherever and whenever ministers were available. Anglicanism as it developed in Virginia, however, was of a distinctly Puritan strain. Although the son of an Archbishop of York, Sir Edwin Sandys, director of the Virginia Company, had studied in Geneva

26

and was a notable leader of the Puritans in Parliament. While he maintained membership in the Church of England and subscribed to the Oath of Supremacy, he also wrote, "if ever God in Heaven did constitute and direct a forme of Government it was that of Geneva." Perry Miller (1970: 35) notes that for the conservative Puritan this did not necessarily indicate a violation of conscience. "Puritans could and did take the oath of supremacy whenever required [unlike most Separatists and later radical sectarians], because it simply bound them to support the forcible establishment of the Church in uniformity throughout the kingdom, and that object they considered laudable. But they had a very concrete idea of what kind of church the oath ought to intend, and this interpretation their opponents could not accept. From the Anglican standpoint there was an element of equivocation in the Puritans' vows, but to the Puritans themselves all was open and aboveboard." This Anglo-Puritan attitude gave a peculiar tinge to Virginia churchmanship that served to buffer the resentment that true Jacobean or Laudian principles and activities might earlier have aroused there. Indeed, at one point part of Sandys' plan was to bring the Separatists (Pilgrims) from Leiden to Virginia. This suggests that his own views may have been even more left-wing than his moderate associates of whom Miller speaks.

Albright (1964: 20-21) further records that a "gentleman bearing letters from Virginia" arrived at Boston as late as 1642 to ask that the New England Puritans supply the Virginians with "faithful ministers." Later in that year, however, the government of Virginia had changed, and the Puritan ministers were ordered to return to their own lands. A fine of £100 was also levied against any shipmaster bringing a Puritan minister into the colony. Soon after this the Assembly passed an act declaring that, "All ministers whatsoever which reside in this Colony are to be conformable to the orders and constitution of the Church of England and the laws therein established; and not otherwise to be admitted to teach or preach publicly or privately." Still, Albright notes that while the required conformity existed at least outwardly among most clergy, neither effective legislation nor a Court of High Commission existed to establish or enforce conformity to an episcopally-oriented point of view, particularly on the part of laymen.[25] This would remain the case throughout the colonial period.

Nevertheless, it was in Virginia, if anywhere, that an attempt was made, at least on paper if not in fact, to reproduce the established church life of England. The southern colonials attempted to recreate the lifestyle of the glorious Elizabethan era immediately past. Yet the facts of life in the new world mandated that this be more a nostalgic dream than a future capable of fulfillment (see Rowse, 1959: 61-88; Brydon, 1947: 40-50, 77-105). In 1641 the Virginia Assembly attempted to organize the colony into parishes akin to those in England, but with vestries governing the local churches. However, the enormous size of the colony and its limited population made impossible the development of a traditional parish community within close range of the church building. Although such factors of southern parochial ecology have long been recognized, they have not really been given attention in colonial church history commensurate with their importance. Not only was the Virginia rector, unlike the New England pastor, thus denied a parish cure similar to that of his homeland, but he was also unable to serve in the same opinion-forming and action-guarding ways he once did (see Herklots, 1966: 32-41).

At the same time, the individualistic, localistic, and mercantile Puritanism that became a part of Virginian Anglicanism made the laity wary of clericalism even at this early date in American history. While Littell (1962: 32) is correct in saying that "there has never been in America an intelligent and coherent anti-clericalism," his observation is only valid in comparing America to other republican countries.[26] Since its earliest years Anglo-America has demonstrated a definite wariness of clerical privilege as it was exercised in (e.g.) Laudian England. Thus Herklots (1966: 40) is equally right when he notes that "The answer to the question why the Episcopal Church in Virginia took so long to recover after the Revolutionary War may . . . be put in a word — anti-clericalism." The clergy, for example, were supposed to be admitted to and share with the vestries in the direction of the life of the parish. Indeed, they were to be the leaders of the vestry. But in practice they were frequently denied this prerogative. Although English canon law forbade prolonged vacancies, in an attempt to maintain local lay control and to keep clerical salaries at a minimum, vestries often refused clergy any but annual appointments. Thus throughout the colonial period, "The Southern Anglicans, especially in Virginia, enjoyed through their vestries a virtually congregational form of church polity, which neither they nor the majority of their parish clergy [who were drawn primarily from the ranks of the right-wing Puritans in England] had any remote desire to change" (Bridenbaugh, 1962: 323; see also 1952: 30-34, 75).

In terms of the model, then, a church-like organization was established in colonial Virginia. Yet it differed in many respects from its mother church across the seas. Unknowingly, the effects of Puritanism's latent pluralism were already making themselves felt (see Sweet, 1935: 43-56). Well over a hundred years would pass before Episcopalianism might be called "denominational"; but the transfer of the monopoly from the office of the (absent) bishop to the (lay) Assembly and vestries signaled an important administrative change that was to have organizational consequences far beyond what could have been imagined at that time. Thus in 1771, Richard Bland, a member of the Virginia House of Burgesses, makes the rather strange assertion, "I profess myself a sincere son of the established church, but I can embrace her Doctrines, without approving of her Hierarchy . . . ." Similarly, in 1774 William Tennent writes from Charleston, South Carolina, to the New England preacher Ezra Stiles that, "The Episcopalians here are highly enraged at your Tory Clergy who are desirous of episcopal principalities, and many of the first of the province do declare to me that they will turn Dissenters in a Body if the Parliament offers to send Bishops over" (in Bridenbaugh, 1962: 322-323). Canon Herklots (1966: 35) summarizes the situation in Virginia by saying, "Virginia was Anglican, but unenthusiastically Anglican." One cannot help but wonder how much of this lack of ardour at the outset contributed also in a latent fashion to the eventual seeming demise of Episcopalianism in this state after the Revolutionary War. What kind of Episcopalians were they who would rather the episcopate were not?

And the Last, First

In many ways the crucial elements of American Anglicanism were provided not in Virginia, with its unenthusiastic established church, but in antagonistic New England, as two other groups came to Massachusetts' shores to try their hands where the earlier Plymouth Company had failed. The first of these were the Pilgrims or Separatists,[27] who followed the congregational teachings of Robert Browne. They had first emigrated from England to Holland to pursue their religious aspirations in an atmosphere of greater toleration. Led by William Bradford, they returned to England and thence set off to the rocky New England coast. The Pilgrims are of interest to this study inasmuch as they were unabashedly congregational in church polity. Their kinship to the English Independents in this regard made them the prime new world practitioners of a critically important form of church government for which these English "dissenting brethren" provided the intellectual underpinnings. This congregationalism sown into American soil by the Pilgrims was to radiate in several different and conflicting directions, but in the end was to provide a basic ingredient for the pluralizing process (see Lipset, 1967: 181).

Clearly exceeding the Pilgrims in overall social impact, however, was the second group of successful Massachusetts *immegrés,* the Puritans. Differing from the Separatists because they maintained their loyalty to the Church of England and expressed a desire to "purify" rather than leave it,[28] the Puritans were the recipients of the brunt of the Laudian advance. Indeed, it may be said that in large part the religion of America as it has unfolded since the seventeenth century is due directly, even if not at all consciously, to the actions of William Laud with regard to the English Puritans. Laud's policy of "Thorough" served to "radicalize the liberal." By insisting on absolute conformity in every detail and by rewarding informers, the Laudians forced many "good Anglicans" into the Puritan camp when their initial convictions may not have been terribly strong either way. G.M. Trevelyan (1954: 173) thus titles Laud "the founder of the Anglo-Saxon supremacy in the New World" (see Bridenbaugh, 1968). John Winthrop, a future governor of the Massachusetts Bay Company colony, affirmed these basic Puritan sentiments in a farewell encomium upon sailing from England in 1630:

> We desire you to take notice of the principals and body of our company, as those who estimate it our honour to call the *Church of England* from whence we rise, our dear Mother . . . ever acknowledging that such hope and part as we have obtained in the common salvation we have received in her bosom, and suckt it from her breasts; we leave it not, therefore, as loathing that milk wherewith we were nourished there, but, blessing God for the parentage and education, as members of the same body, shall always rejoice in her good, and unfeignedly grieve for any sorrow that shall ever betide her, and while we have breath, sincerely desire and endeavor the continuance and abundance of her welfare [in Morgan, 1958: 53].

Although Jessett (1952: 306) argues that the "dear mother" references evidence "a sentimental rather than a logical attitude" on Winthrop's part, the fact that the "Anglicans" of this ilk were subsequently absorbed into the congregationalism that was a part of Separatist doctrine should not call into question the sincerity of their original intentions. The Puritan Francis Higginson, for example, claimed "We do not go to New England as Separatists from the Church of England, though we cannot but separate from the corruptions in it" (in Selbie, 1912: 64). Different material conditions may entail different value positions. Sweet (1965: 84) comments:

> The difference between Pilgrim and Puritan toward the Church of England and the royal authority may thus be summarized: The Pilgrims repudiated the Church of England in all its parts, but recognized the King as their royal [temporal] master [because their theology made a clear separation between church and state]; the Puritans desired to

build a state without a king [the Genevan form], and rejected as far as they dared the royal authority [and with it all forms of episcopal hierarchy], but the English Church they recognized as their "dear mother" in all things spiritual . . .

Because of the intertwining of church and state, a principle the Puritans accepted when they left England, church government was a political rather than a spiritual matter to the Puritans. Thus they could reject episcopal supervision and still maintain spiritual loyalty. Save for the changes of polity that were made as the Puritans established themselves in New England, and for the differing ecological and geographical patterns that developed in the North and the South, the Anglicanism established in Virginia and the Puritan "Anglicanism" established in New England were but two slightly different shades of a single-colored phenomenon (see Miller, 1956b: 99-140; Bellah, 1975). Both were "so transformed as to exclude what were to become the most characteristic marks of Anglicanism" (Herklots, 1966: 18), and in both were the latent tendencies that would lead to the breakdown of their tenuous monopolies and the restructuring of the entire social system.

What Bridenbaugh (1968: 4, 434-473) terms "the Puritan Hegira" began "in 1607 as a mere trickle, increased to a recognizable stream after 1620, and after 1629 became a mighty flood." Archbishop Laud was hardly unaware of this exodus when he was translated to Canterbury in 1633, nor was he willing to see Puritanism become established anywhere that the flag of his sovereign was flying. "Break unity once," he warned, "and farewell strength" (in Miller, 1970: 12). He intended that every Englishman should have the ministrations of a Church of England clergyman *ipso facto* under the authority of an English bishop and none other. In Elizabethan and Jacobean times Englishmen abroad went with royal approbation "to that very worship which Elizabeth and James persecuted at home." With Charles this practice was disallowed, and Englishmen "beyond the seas" were required to conform to the Church of England (Macaulay, 1967: II 60). Early in his primary, Laud made efforts to see that the colonists in "foreign parts" should not be allowed to fall from "ye liturgy and discipline now used in ye Church of England," as they seemed all too prone to do. The Archbishop first attempted to control the American branch of the English Church by securing the right to establish a governing board for the colonies, which would consist of twelve members, Lords Temporal and Spiritual. These, or any five of them, were given monopolistic "power for the rule and protection of the colonies" in both political and, in consultation with two or three additional bishops, ecclesiastical affairs. They were also given the power to inflict punishments so that their directives would be heeded. In short, they were endowed with virtually supreme control over every possible branch of colonial affairs, and were accountable only to the King in one of many royal "monopolies."

A second like commission was issued to Laud two years later. In spite of these directives, however, the emigration to New England continued to mount, as did the stringency of the Laudian project at home. Alarmed by this, the Archbishop prompted the King to issue a proclamation that none should pass to New England "without license from the commissioners of the several ports, and a testimony from their ministers of their conformity to the order and discipline of their church," which Laud clearly understood to mean *his* Church. In addition, a second proclamation was issued requiring that clergy going to the American colonies must have a testimonial from both the Archbishop of Canterbury and the Bishop of London. Formerly the latter alone, having traditional jurisdiction for Anglicans outside the country, would have provided this document. This proclamation evidences Laud's desire to have a personal hand in colonial affairs. The whole scheme was generally ineffectual, however, since the New Englanders did not believe in episcopal ordination and were quite willing to provide for themselves, opening Harvard in 1636.

As a final step to insure the success of his plan, Laud made arrangements in 1638 to send a bishop to America. Various interferences, particularly trouble in Scotland and the Short and Long Parliaments at home, prolonged the consecration and thus the realization of the plan until the Puritan revolution, when Laud's own demise also dashed these efforts. Nonetheless, this was the first attempt in the Church of England to provide a bishop for the New World in an effort to maintain the royal monopoly (see A.L. Cross, 1964: 19-21).

It was undoubtedly incomprehensible to Laud that the Church could function without a bishop, or that the government of England could be maintained in the colonies without the episcopacy being present to extend its "sacred canopy" over the lives of His Majesty's subjects. In a round-about way, of course, he was quite right. The absence of the Church of England hierarchy may well have been one of the most important factors leading to American independence. Consider, for example, the views of Thomas Bradbury Chandler, a protagonist of the American episcopate and Anglican missionary in New Jersey. In 1766, following the Stamp Act riots in the colonies, he wrote to his superiors in England:

> If ye interest of the Church of England in America had been made a National Concern from the beginning, by this time a general submission in ye Colonies to ye Mother Country in everything not sinful might have been expected . . . Indeed, many wise and good persons, at home, have had ye Cause of Religion and ye Church here sincerely at heart . . . who by their indefatigable endeavors to *propogate the Gospel* and assist the Church, have, at the same time, and thereby secured to ye State, as far as their influence could be extended, ye Loyalty and Fidelity of her American Children [in A.L. Cross, 1964: 113-114, see also 165-167, 251].

The message of Chandler and his contemporaries for us is clear. The monarchy and the church were so interwoven that if the religious organization were not present in America as in England, the monarchy's monopoly would crumble, as in fact it did. The perceived importance of the *absence* of an Anglican episcopate to colonial society is the subject of Bridenbaugh's *Mitre and Sceptre* (1962; see A.L. Cross, 1964, Mills, 1978). Particularly relevant in terms of the model is the importance of the interaction effects between church and society. While the seventeenth century Church of England was clearly a political creation in many critical respects, the monarchy's perpetuation seems in turn to have become dependent upon the religious organization. A dialectic is thus in evidence.

This chronicle of the reigns of the English monarchs from Henry VIII through Charles I demonstrates the extent to which the Church of England was thoroughly monopolistic in structure and function. Yet we also note the growth of a countermovement. Advanced initially to curb ecclesiastical abuses, *Puritanism* was developing into something far more extensive, with far greater changes to come in its wake. The next chapter provides a more detailed look at the Puritan ideology and the structural effects that lay within it.

Chapter 3
THE PURITAN IDEOLOGY, PLURALISM, AND DENOMINATIONALISM

What Goes Up . . .

As the number of entrenched sect-like Puritans increased to parallel the "thoroughness" of Laud's "reform," the monopoly stood at a tenuous high. The Carolines had theologized and politicked the Elizabethan Settlement to the breaking point. The popular element implicit in the notion of King-in-Parliament was absent. On the organizational level, neither church nor state encompassed English society. The "beginning of the end" for the church-like position of Anglicanism, as well as of the patrimonial monopoly upon which the Stuart government rested, occurred in 1640 when Parliament was twice called into session. The first of these assemblies was the Short Parliament. It angered Charles and after a few days was prorogued. At this time whenever Parliament met, Convocation, the bishops and clerical deputies that "ruled" the Church of England, was also convened. Contrary to accepted custom, however, when this session of Parliament was suspended, Convocation continued to meet and passed a collection of seventeen canons to intertwine further Laudian churchmanship and the Caroline monarchy. These canons did exactly what they were supposed to do and, in effect, sealed the doom of the Episcopal monopoly.

> The first canon declares that "the most high and sacred order of Kings is of Divine right, being the ordinance of God Himself, founded in the prime laws of nature and clearly established by express texts of both the Old and New Testaments." A further canon, No. 6, sought to impose upon the clergy, schoolmasters and others an oath, known as the "etcetera Oath" which contained the words: "Nor will I ever give my consent to alter the government of this Church by archbishops, bishops, deans and archdeacons, etc. as it stands now established." This oath caused great offence since the vague word "etc." might open the door to all kinds of innovations in Church government to which the swearer of the oath would have committed himself [Moorman, 1963: 228].

Continuing difficulties at home and abroad forced Charles to reassemble Parliament later in the year, thus beginning the Long Parliament. In December this body received the *Root and Branch Petition,* a document supposedly endorsed by 15,000 Londoners demanding the abolition, "root and branch," of government by archbishops, bishops, deans, and archdeacons. In effect, it demanded a dismantling of the entire organizational structure of the Church of England. A week after this petition was received William Laud was impeached and imprisoned. In spite of some self-serving vacillation after Laud's incarceration, the bishops lost their seats in Lords in 1642 (see J. Hall, 1952). "For Anglicans," Lamont (1969: 78) observes, "the crucial happening in 1641 was the destruction of Laudianism." This point marks the movement of the Church of England from "church-like" to "established sect-like" in terms of the model. While the "Establishment" would retain its official status and episcopacy for several years, it had clearly lost the English people. It was, thus, no longer a monopolistic institution but, rather, an inapposite vestige established (in this case) by religio-cultural lag in a society seething with revolution. This analysis is confirmed by the presentation of the *Grand Remonstrance* from Parliament to Charles listing its grievances against King, court, and clergy. As Moorman notes (1963: 228-229), "Clauses 181-204 deal with religion and include a demand for the reduction of the power of the bishops, for the holding of a synod to which foreign Protestants should be invited, and for steps to be taken to remove 'idolatrous and Popish ceremonies introduced into the Church by the command of the Bishops'. Charles, infuriated by this, and encouraged by the [Roman Catholic] queen, outraged the privileges of Parliament by entering the House of Commons and attempting to arrest five members."

In a year when Independent preachers were already proclaiming King Jesus as "the sole anointed King of his church" and "the one and only King of saints" (see Tolmie, 1977: 85-94), Charles never gained the support he had hoped such a rash measure would produce. Rather, the event occasioned the distribution of Henry Walker's tract *To Your Tents O Israel!*, one of the first pieces of printed material to call for the rejection of Charles' kingship. In 1642 Parliament declared of itself, "What they do herein hath the stamp of the royal authority although his majesty, seduced by evil counsel, do in his own person oppose or interrupt the same" (see Cantor, 1967; Hexter, 1941). Plummer (1904: 138-139) remarks that "Parliament was now the sovereign of its sovereign Charles." If Charles would not capitulate to Parliament's demands, war remained the only course of action. "The question of the Divine Right of Kings was to be submitted to the ordeal of battle" (Moorman, 1963: 229).

The Great Rebellion that terminated all of Laud's plans for an American episcopate was an attempt on the part of Englishmen to gain their civil liberties. It was ostensibly a war of religion, a war against episcopacy, autocracy, "spiritual wickedness in high places," and the doctrine of the Divine Right of Kings. But it was also a struggle for every person to have a hand in deciding the policies of the country as they affected everyday life.[1] Thus, under the circumstances in which church-state relationships were conceived, "Puritanism was the only available ideology that could effectively legitimize opposition to church and state simultaneously" (Israel, 1966: 591).[2]

To the seventeenth-century English people, religion and politics were inseparable intertwined. It was a century that "often argued in religious terms when it was actually concerned with political ends" (Jordan, 1942): 67). This does not mean that these times were better nor the people more religious, "But it does mean that religious categories were regarded as more important than they are nowadays" (Yule, 1958: 2). The "double character" of the "intimate connexion between politics and religion" in seventeenth century England created a web of relationships that represented an English everyday view-of-life and carried with it a symbolic universe of meaning (see Wakeman, 1887: 90). "Puritanism scored heavily with those Englishmen who were intensely nationalistic, for, unlike

Anglicanism, Puritanism was blatantly anti-Roman Catholic . . . For some Englishmen, Protestantism and patriotism were virtually indistinguishable" (Israel, 1966: 592). It is, thus, woefully inadequate to view religious expression and language merely as a facade for the "real" underlying political and economic convictions of the seventeenth-century Englishman. In this sense, religious expression was much more sacramental. It was both sign *and* means.

The Presbyterian support forthcoming from the Scots, however, was no more what the English wanted than was the earlier Episcopacy. The famous aphorism of John Milton (whose sympathies were clearly Independent), "New Presbyter is but old Priest writ large," testifies to this. Many who had willingly supported the destruction of the despotism of the Caroline monopoly found only a new form of tyranny in the right-wing Presbyterians who gained ascendancy as the Rebellion brewed. There was no more liberty under the one order than the other (see Miller, 1970: 15-52; Trevor-Roper, 1972: 392-444). Thus, "in 1645, the very year in which Presbyterianism was proclaimed the state religion [in England], the ascendancy of the Presbyterians came to an end" (Gooch, 1954: 105). The dedication of right-wing Puritanism (i.e. Presbyterianism) to the continuation of monopolistic principles provoked the rise of the Independents, the heirs of Separatism. In their zeal for personal liberty, and with the support of Oliver Cromwell, they attempted to set the Church free.[3] The structural consequences of this state of affairs for religious organization was a situation of nascent denominationalism. Accordingly, Puritanism, as a vehicle of religio-social change, becomes a major variable in this analysis.

Clarifying the Puritan Ideology

Like most "isms," Puritanism is subject to a variety of contradictory meanings. Leonard Trinterud observes that "There was something odd about the English Puritans. On that, everyone seems to have been in agreement for the last four hundred years" (1971: 3). Saint-Just grasped its double potential when he defined it as "Either virtue or a reign of terror" (in Lipset, 1964: 117). Certainly for some, Puritanism is the bearer of freedom, the great heritage of a free society. Others see Puritanism as repressive and having strongly negative connotations. Some interpret Puritanism as a purely theological phenomenon. Others treat theology as epiphenomenon and insist that Puritanism is but a language form for a particular economic system. From one point of view Puritanism is the direct antecedent of rationalism. From another, it is the height of irrationality. Some see Puritanism as the basis for mutual love among Christians of varying backgrounds. More argue that its unrelenting demand for perfection on minute points of doctrine and morality has caused denominational proliferation and religious conflict. But this much is sure: "Puritanism, not the Tudor secession from Rome, was the true English Reformation, and it is from its struggle against the old order that an England which is unmistakeably modern emerges" (Tawney, 1960: 199). Because Puritanism is so important to the sociological analysis of the interactions considered here, we must have a clear understanding of what it is (see Little, 1969: 226-236; 250-259).

A critical defining concept in Israel's assessment of the success of Puritanism is that it was an "ideology,"[4] something that develops out of and subsequently contains the concrete workings of a sociocultural unit and is thus primarily *social* in character. In this sense it stands opposed to *theoria,* abstract analyses of the mind that remain relatively unconnected to the workings of every-day life. If we properly understand the seventeenth century, this quality is grasped fully by David Hall's claim (1972) that Puritanism is "pastoral theology *writ large.*" Such an understanding should dispel a purely theological conception of Puritanism as an intra-ecclesiastical reform movement or theory of church government. John Calvin is, of course, rightly considered to have provided the theological or doctrinal base for Puritanism, but Puritanism is much more than Calvinism. It includes pieces of Calvin's doctrine, but also adds a number of other assertions about such things as the rights of man, individual initiative, the nature of law, and the right workings of an economic system. As Little (1969: 33-80) points out in his treatment of Calvin's work, there are ambiguities in his writings, and much can be imputed to him unless the corpus is taken as a whole and ap-parent contradictions placed into perspective. Perhaps we do best to say with Haller (1938: 84-85) that the Puritans were "Calvinists with a difference."[5]

The basic work here remains Max Weber's *Protestant Ethic and the Spirit of Capitalism,* particularly the essay of 1905. While this is not the place for a thoroughgoing discussion of Weber's thesis, much of the work on Weber misunderstands what he was about here (however, see B. Nelson, 1973). Although it is true that Calvin's system and Baxter's Puritanism are not identical, Weber never said they were. What he did say is that Puritanism is peculiarly rooted and grounded in the Genevan ideal, and that this aspect of Puritanism made a substantial contribution to the development of "rational capitalism." On the other hand, it is a mistake to redefine Calvinism (as Walzer [1966: 22] does) so that it becomes synonymous with the Puritan ideology. The line that Weber draws from Calvin's theology to English Puritanism clearly exists (via the Marian exiles), but Weber never intended that the two be considered isomorphic. I would say with Forcese (1968; also see Merton, 1970: vii-xxix) that: "It is our contention that the Weberian thesis has been done an injustice . . . Weber's intention was to demonstrate a relationship between Calvinism and a peculiar form of capitalism, not in terms of genesis, but in terms of 'feedback' [i.e. interaction]."

As an ideology, Puritanism will vary from place to place and time to time as the numerous possible implications of that ideology are realized by the people themselves: "It is unnecessary to posit a *unity* in all Puritan thought; it is suffi-cient to recognize a continuity. Puritanism means a determined and varied effort to erect a holy community and to meet, with different degrees of compromise and adjustment, the problem of its conflict with the world" (Woodhouse, 1974: 37). The result is that the ultimate consequences of the Puritan ideology may or may not resemble the life style of the people who were giving shape to it. "The true nature of the Reformation," like most social movements, "is found not in its in-tention but in its result" (Gooch, 1954: 1). Likewise there will be debates about the meanings of the ideology that will be finally settled only in specific historical events. Thus, to understand the meaning and development of an ideology, it must be studied in the historical context in which it was born and then matured.

Puritanism cannot be equated simply with the Knoxian reformation in Scotland and the establishment of Calvinism there. Knoxian Presbyterianism was a theological scheme for church government that engulfed Scotland and carried Puritanism with it in its wake (see Jordan, 1965: 274-316). The suddenness with which the Scottish reformation occurred, and its close attachment to a single powerful figure, provided little chance for the Puritan ideology to develop there as it did in England. Establishment stifled the freedom of thought that could continue elsewhere. Thus the Presbyterian-Puritan establishment in Scotland became extremely monopolistic in character ("church-like") and was quite late to recognize the place of liberty in the Puritan ideology. Rather than undoing the Church of Scotland, Presbyterianism became the Church of Scotland.

In terms of the model, the Scottish case exhibits almost no initial movement at the systemic level. Knox returned to Scotland from the continent and with remarkable speed instituted a new dogma which, instead of leading to significant sociocultural change, was actually incorporated into a progravid social system. Thus he created a new monopoly serving ends already latent in Scottish society. The Knoxian theocracy functioned in like manner to Henrican Erastianism. Both met pre-existing needs in the larger social system. In each case church and state formed a union, accepting one another. Puritanism in Scotland (better, perhaps, Knoxianism) was never placed in an entrenched sect-like position out of which it had to change the world. In England, on the other hand, Puritanism's inner-worldly character forced it to act in just this way. Ironically, if James I had sanctioned and established Presbyterianism as it existed in his native Scotland, the full flowering of the Puritan ideology might have been severely retarded. His decision to bolster the episcopal hierarchy and his own monopoly further and his refusal to hear the pleas of the Puritans forced them into the entrenched sect-like beginnings that were realized by the Laudian policy. This meant that given the inner-worldly character of Puritanism, the Stuart monopoly had to be toppled. Although the monopoly-oriented Knoxians made valiant tries at complete control before Cromwell succeeded in bringing down the monopoly, they were continually frustrated and remained in an established sect-like position. "Here we have an argument we shall encounter frequently: Initial receptivity of a system to new forms does not lead to gradual continuous change but rather to the stifling of the change, whereas initial resistance often leads later on to a breakthrough" (Wallerstein, 1974: 59).

The Presbyterian party began something in Parliament that could not be contained there:[6] "In England the royal and Anglican policy was broken down by the Puritans under the Long Parliament. Their struggle with the king was pursued for decades under the war cry 'down with the monopolies' which were granted in part to foreigners and in part to courtiers, while the colonies were placed in the hands of royal favorites. The extraordinary obstinacy with which the economic spirit of the English people has striven against trusts and monopolies is expressed in these Puritan struggles" (Weber, 1950: 257).[7] As Parliamentarians and barristers argued against monopoly in trade, so Puritans with a more radical vision argued against it in religion. "Of all Monopolies or Patents," said the Leveller John Lilburne, "the monopolizing of ingrossing the Preaching of Gods Word into the Tything and gripeing clawes of the Clergy . . . is the most wicked and intollerable." Henry Robinson likewise argued that "Men should be free to buy truth where it suits them best," and asked, "Would not the encroachments of the Church in any other trade, be damned for a monopoly — the 'greatest infringing of the Subjects property'?" (in Little, 1969: 256-257).[8]

What, then, was it that turned the people toward "left wing" Puritanism and caused the rejection of a Presbyterian establishment?[9] The answer is complex and involves the interaction of intellectual, social, political, and economic circumstances which led to open and active criticism of both the monarchy and religious authoritarianism. Projected into this was the Puritan ideology, and particularly a sense of the freedom of the individual to work out his own salvation "in fear and trembling." First, then, the most right-wing Puritan elements were still protesting that they were the real Church of England, just as the Knoxians were the Church of Scotland. The Presbyterians, while preaching against the power and prestige of the Episcopal establishment, demanded the same power for themselves. The question of the tenability of the very idea of monopoly was not being confronted (see Crowley, 1973). The Parliamentary debates were carried on by the representatives of the more well-to-do members of the commercial class with little direct concern for the workingman (see Brunton & Pennington, 1954). Similarly, the most articulate Presbyterian spokesmen were seldom heard by the working class. The latter had to be content with finding one of their own station gifted in oratory and with some ability to read. They could then ordain him in their own congregation. Finally, while the Westminster Assembly, called to create a Puritan establishment, became lost in theological details, a soldier named Cromwell was taking his Independent Puritan teaching to heart and changing the everyday world of England.[10]

> By the end of 1644 the divines of the assembly had failed to silence opposition in the press as completely as they had failed to secure agreement among the members of their own order. The Independent minority in the assembly still held out against centralized control over individual preachers and congregations . . . The preachers had done their pulpit-work well, but with practical results that few of them had looked for and many of them deplored. They had sown the Word without foreseeing the harvest they had now to reap. They had preached the doctrines of calling and covenant, evinced by faith, manifested in action, to be crowned by success here or hereafter, and they had thus planted in many minds dreams of a new heaven and new earth. But *it is one thing to launch men on a quest for the New Jerusalem, quite another to stop them when they have gone far enough* . . . Hence all attempts in 1644 to impose a Presbyterian frame upon revolutionary Puritanism served simply to evoke the many-headed hydra of English dissent [Haller, 1955: 141-142, italics mine].

Puritanism as ideology won the day over Presbyterianism as an ecclesiastical theory of government because Puritanism grew from a voluntaristic base in English society. As Little (1969: 94-95) notes in his summation of the Puritan Thomas Cartwright's writings on ecclesiastical and civil authority, "Only in voluntary consent can true order be achieved. Consent is the glue of the Body." Such a political philosophy was clearly different from that of the Knoxians (see Walzer, 1966: 104-109). Faced with intolerable odds by the Laudian project, the entrenched sect-like Puritans came to know the power of voluntary commitment in religion. They then transferred this new type of social structure over to the political institution:

> Perhaps the most significant thing about Puritan democratic theory is that the Puritans began with the experience of working in a small and thoroughly democratic society, the Puritan congregation. Their idea of a church is that it is a fellowship of active believers. The self-governing congregation was for them the church. In such a society all are equal, in the sense . . . that they were all equally called of God. That fundamental fact outweighed their differences of ability, capacity, character, and

wealth so completely that these differences could be freely recognized and made use of. The Puritan congregation is a fellowship of equals who are recognized to be different. They are all alike called by God and guided by him, and therefore all equally called on to contribute to the common discussion about the purpose and actions of their small society — a society which did not use force in the putting into practice of its decisions, but was a fellowship of discussion. Because [in England] the Puritan tradition started with the experience of a society which rested on consent and abjured the use of force, it tended to conceive the state on the analogy of such a society [Lindsay, 1962: 117-118].

The Cromwellian victory gave vent to the full force of the Puritan spirit for the first time in English history (see Perry, 1944). "Right down to 1640 men could not be sure that Protestantism had come to stay in England" (C. Hill, 1967: 49). Yet one must not overrate the immediate consequences of the Protectorate. The Rebellion did, of course, abolish episcopacy, organs, altars, vestments, the hierarchical system, imposed rites and ceremonies (the *Book of Common Prayer*), and in short, anything associated with traditional English churchmanship. All this plus the martyrdom of King Charles suggests a triumph (albeit brief) for the forces of religious liberty. I prefer, however, to see this as *nascent* denominationalism, a bringing-to-birth rather than a completion of the process. While it is true that the government of 1650 found it difficult to insure the carrying out of Sunday observance, even here there was an insistance that the people be bound into a community of faith (see C. Cross, 1972; Jordan, 1965: III 119-170; Williams, 1930). No *particular* public confession of doctrine was necessary. Yet the 1653 Instrument of Government that extended toleration made it clear that one must "profess faith in God by Jesus Christ" and that there were limits: "this liberty be not extended to popery or prelacy" (see Moorman, 1963: 244). Thus the liberty of toleration rather than the liberty of pluralism first manifested itself at this point in English history. As Coolidge (1970: 26) notes, though "liberty" is at the center of the Puritan-Anglican controversies, the concept must not be viewed in a twentieth-century light: "The Puritan thinks of Christian liberty less as a permission than as a command. To do 'any of those things which God hath not commanded' [e.g. kneel at Communion or wear a surplice] would be, not an assertion but a violation of Christian liberty."[11]

In terms of the model, there were two important developments during this period. On the one hand, the Church of England "moved" from an established sect-like position to an entrenched sect-like status. Although this was a gradual process, it is marked by the execution of Laud and the abolition of episcopacy in 1644-1645. Its confirmation is found in the decollation of Charles in 1649 (see Watson, 1972; Wedgwood, 1964: 106-187; and Hutton, 1913: 36-98, 122-178). The monopoly was utterly vanquished. The attempt to abolish every possible artifact of traditional English churchmanship and the derogatory appelation "prelacy" are further evidences of the "underground" status that its faithful members and ministers would have to bear. On the other hand, there was an even more important consequence of the Rebellion, the open appearance of independent established sects. The government of Cromwell, by failing to embrace any particular religious party, affirmed the doctrine of the Church Invisible (but with Visible Saints) and with it, the right of Protestants to worship as they pleased. Preexistent in the underground tradition, the sects now blossomed forth and multiplied (see Watts, 1978; Worden, 1974; Gooch, 1954: 228-238).

What happened in England at the mid-point of the seventeenth century was not without consequences for her American colonies. Many of these consequences were indirect results of *in*activity in the mother country regarding the colonial religious situation. The two decades surrounding the martyrdom of King Charles were the most formative for the shaping of America's religious life. In a word, what did *not* happen in America at this time was "bishops." I propose to explore here by means of the model the significance of this absence, which meant the effectual absence of an action-system to enforce the English episcopal-monarchial monopoly in America.

In the last chapter, I noted the transformation in the religious life of Virginia Anglicanism that was present almost from the settling of that colony and that persisted throughout the colonial period and the early days of the new republic (see Eckenrode, 1971). The failure to send a bishop to the colony previous to the protectorate permitted what might have been a temporary deviation to become much more ingrained in the life of Virginia churchmen. Although efforts were made following the Restoration to return the Virginians to "normal" Anglicanism, none was successful.[12] Only after the conclusion of the War of Independence and disestablishment in Virginia, when Anglicanism there reached a low ebb, was regularized Episcopalianism accepted. The failure of a bishop to arrive in Virginia resulted in the type of Anglicanism established there being far from a powerful hierarchical monopoly. Virginia clearly had an established Protestant Christianity ("church-type" in the model), but it was localistic and lacked the presence of the "priest royal" with monarchically appointed courts to uphold undeviating conformity to "official" doctrine, discipline, and worship. The *mysterium tremendum* of ecclesiastical power was lost in England's revolutionary shuffle. The main consequences examined in this chapter, however, are those in New England and, to a lesser extent, the middle-Atlantic states. There are two basic divisions into which these may be grouped: first, the embracing of Congregationalism by the Puritan immigrants and its establishment in New England, and second, the development of the anti-Episcopal mythology which Bridenbaugh terms the "Great Fear."

The Congregational Way

The Puritans leaving England to form the Massachusetts Bay Colony were adherents to quasi-Presbyterian political sentiments. They left their homeland protesting their loyalty to the Church of England, that needed only to be properly purified. Although it is a matter of debate among historians,[13] the details surrounding the ecclesiastical maneuverings of these New England settlers, their dissenting brethren at home, and the Pilgrims at Plymouth is unimportant here. What *is* important is that the Congregational Way was adopted and established by the New England Puritans and officially embodied in the Cambridge Platform of 1648 (see D. Hall, 1972: 93-120).

The problem of order was the focal point for religious controversy in this period. The Puritan ideology spoke directly to it by celebrating "liberty to do good" — i.e., to follow the Anglo-Calvinist version of the biblical pattern of living "literally."[14] But New England also presented a challenge to the English Puritans that would have to be met if their "liberty" were to be maintained. The voluntary puritan society had to incorporate *control* in a way previously unknown. If reports of a disordered people should return to the mother country, royal and episcopal intrusion might well result. But, as Bushman (1970: 147) notes, "The Congregational polity in England was at first designed not to sustain a social order but to disrupt one." The Independents were trying to rid themselves of any authority beyond that of the local covenanted congregation. In attacking the episcopal hierarchy, they also struck a sizeable blow to external authority in general. In America, on the other hand, "Congregationalism had to transform its polity from an instrument of rebellion to one of control. The church carried the responsibility of subduing men to the social order." The voluntarism of the Puritan congregation meant that technically only those who willingly consented could come under discipline. Yet every boatload from England brought both "saints" and "sinners." Furthermore, once settlers had been here for some time, a new generation of adults might or might not choose to accept the covenant and its discipline. Ways had to be found to extend discipline beyond the voluntary congregation. The result, Bushman continues, was that "clerical authority was enlarged and consolidated at the expense of the powers of the congregation. As a result, a century after settlement Congregationalism had reverted to many practices of the very Establishment the Puritans had once sought to escape." Thus Robert Pope in his book *The Half-Way Covenant* (1969) sees this "mode of membership" alteration in New England Congregationalism as a means of adapting to the need for order in that social system. In regard to the model, this is one of the kinds of belief-system alterations that may be necessary in internal organizational change, e.g., rejection to acceptance (see J.W. Jones, 1973; Boyer & Nissenbaum, 1974).

The over-riding concern of the sixteenth and seventeenth centuries with the "law and order" question is the basis of David Little's *Religion, Order, and Law,* and it is not necessary to repeat Little's exposition of the topic in detail. He observes that Anglo-American society was moving from monopolism to pluralism via the medium of the Puritan ideology, and that this metamorphosis was neither a simple nor linear process. He continually stresses that there were marked ambiguities and dilemmas which took time to resolve; yet:

The kind of practical accommodation achieved with the political-legal authorities will [inversely] determine to a great extent how intensely and how novelly the characteristic of ascetic Protestantism will be expressed, and . . . the kind of political accommodation depends in large measure upon historical circumstance . . . . If the political order is successfully subordinated to the theological purposes of Reformed faith . . . the distinctiveness of the new order — including its ingredients of voluntarism, universalism, modification of political control, and so on — will not be so intensely or novelly expressed (though they will not by any means be altogether eliminated either) . . . [Puritanism] is not "merely" the function of a social situation — a phenomenon that looks one way in one situation and quite the opposite in another. It is a coherent phenomenon that moves in determinate directions depending, in part, on the social situation [1969: 129].

Thus, the Presbyterian-Puritan establishment in Scotland became extremely monopolistic and was quite late to recognize the place of liberty in the Puritan ideology. When Congregationalism came to be the Way of New England, the order question posed a real dilemma. It was much easier to advance rather radical notions about liberty when the established Church of England was at hand with all of its apparatus to legitimize punitive government, maintain social control, and provide a comprehensive plausibility structure that would justify all sorts of everyday injustices.

The New England errand faced the Puritans with the practical matters of creating and maintaining a social structure under their own guidance without the imposed constraints provided by the religio-social establishment of the mother country. "Our forefathers," as the first settlers came soon to be known (see Bridenbaugh, 1962: 173-174), found a patchwork of Calvinistic theology and democratic process to be a temporary solution to their problem (see Bushman, 1970: 5-18; Miller, 1961a). Elections, rather than expressing the "will of the people," were more like the casting of lots, a means by which God made His will known to His people. In the Calvinistic system all things exist to glorify God. His will is immutable and all-righteous. Man is a sinner and incapable of doing any good without God. Therefore all good comes from God. Any evil in government is the result of man's sinfulness or the work of the devil. Since God is always in complete command of the universe, He uses even this to test, to winnow, and so further magnify His glory through the praise and virtue of the elect. Thus, the deity himself was the monarch of the Puritan monopoly. The covenanted brethren but exercised his sovereign will revealed to them through the Scriptures interpreted at the hand of the "chosen and called" ministers.

Sweet (1965: 88) provides a succinct outline of the New England Puritan "reasoning" upon which such arguments rested:

(1) The Scriptures are definitive for doctrine, polity and government. (2) They are so plainly written that "he that runneth may read." (3) Dissenters [from the Puritan Way] are those who misinterpret or misunderstand the Scriptures, and are in error for that reason. (4) It is the duty of the minister to show dissenters where they are in error . . . (5) Then, if the dissenter still failed to agree, it was not because the Scriptures were not plain enough, but because he wilfully persisted in error against the light of his own conscience [what Puritan gnosticism (see Voegelin, 1957) termed "will worship"]. Thus John Cotton held that it was wrong to persecute a man against conscience, but argued that no man's conscience compelled him to reject the truth, and therefore to force the truth upon him was no violation of conscience.

Jessett (1952: 308) notes the response of William Blaxton, who abandoned Massachusetts for Rhode Island: "I came from England, because I did not like the lord-bishops; but I cannot join with you, because I would not be under the lord-brethren."[15]

Thus the Congregational Way was established and expressed in the Cambridge Platform of 1648. Prelacy and popery were contrary to the Word of God and would not be permitted in the New Jerusalem. Presbyteries could not be proved unquestionably from Scripture. The only form of polity clearly scriptural to the New Englander was Congregationalism, where each congregation had its "bishops," all were priests, and some (the deacons) were set apart to "wait tables."[16] Since this was the only church polity to be proved from the "plain Word of Scripture," the "true Way" could not merely be left to chance. The elect must foster the command of the Almighty. Congregationalism had to be established by law so that those who had not yet been converted to the Way might still hear God's call, or if eternally reprobate, might not keep the righteous from encountering the Divine Presence or observing God's Laws. "Democracy," wrote John Cotton to Lord Say, "I do not conceive God ever did ordain as a fit government, either for Church or Commonwealth. If the People be governors, who shall be governed?

As for Monarchy and Aristocracy, they are both clearly approved and directed in Scripture, yet so as referreth the sovereignty to Himself and setteth up theocracy in both as the best form of government in the Commonwealth as in the Church." To Roger Williams, he wrote, "That is a civil law whatsoever concerneth the good of the city . . . now religion is the best good of the city, and therefore laws concerning religion are truly civil laws." As Gooch (1954: 68-69) remarks, "The vital principle of true Independency, the separation of Church and State, is missing." Thus a rationale externally dissimilar to that offered by sixteenth-century Anglicanism yields the same result, a rigid monopolistic establishment with a church-like religious organization.

There were, however, certain differences in the two establishments that are worth noticing for their impact upon future developments in each sociocultural system. First, the Anglican system was hierarchical and centralized. The American situation was far more localistic. The Anglican rationale placed supremacy in the single figure of the King. Any change in the Anglican patrimonial system entailed a change in both the institution of the monarchy and the person of the monarch himself. Furthermore, any diminution of the monarch's powers tended to be also a diminution of the powers of the Church. As a result, whole new conceptions of the numinous were required, or religion was to endure a serious blow to its power as a social force. In America, on the other hand, the latency of Puritanism acted as a restraining force to prevent the wholesale decline of religious expression as pluralistic tendencies increased (see Lipset, 1967: 180-182). By viewing the "true Church" as that known only to God and temporally composed of "visible saints," account could also be taken of human error without the church's credibility suffering. The absence of traditional sanctions for the New England establishment combined with the openendedness of Puritan individualism made possible a hermaneutics under whose egis tergiversation without incredulity was given a viability that it never could have had in post-Laudian England. The Puritan election, for example, could be much more easily turned from an expression of the will of God to one of the will of the people, than could the doctrine of Divine Right (see Miller, 1956b: 2-15; Bushman, 1970: 149-220; and Marty, 1969: 98-104).

The Fear

A concomitant of the Congregational establishment in New England was the development of the "Great Fear," the anti-episcopal myth that worked to keep English bishops out of her colonies until after the Revolutionary War. The myth grew out of the Laudian oppression of the Puritans. Its tenets are: Our forefathers sought the liberty to worship God in the way He ordained. They could not do so in England and were severely persecuted by bishops. Enduring many great perils, they came to this New World "wilderness" that Christianity might be practiced in its biblical purity. Bishops are unchristian men, "ravening wolves in sheep's clothing," using the cruel powers of the state in the guise of the Gospel to destroy the true worship of God. If bishops were ever to come to the New World, they would deprive us of both our liberty to worship and our money. In order to live in luxurious palaces, they would oppress honest working men and tillers of the soil. Whenever a bishop is present, liberty will be absent. Thus the myth recounted from generation to generation the oppressive monopoly that prelacy had once had over the lives and liberties of good Christian men and women.

A first result of the establishment myth in the Puritan-dominated New England region was that Anglicanism became a despised and oppressed minority. "In all New England in 1690, only at Boston did a Church of England congregation exist. There the Anglicans were the 'dissenters' and indeed they were made to feel so" (Bridenbaugh, 1962: 56). Until well into the eighteenth century Anglicans in New England (Rhode Island excepted) were required to pay taxes for the support of the Congregationalist pastor and meetinghouse (see Tyng, 1960: 6-32; Jessett, 1952: 309-315). Only as penalties were lifted from the shoulders of other "dissenters" by the Congregationalists did the Anglicans begin to feel relief as well. Anglicanism was unquestionably an entrenched sect in the early Puritan society. Thus, Samuel Seabury, the first Anglican bishop to serve in the New World, remarked in 1790 that the early Congregationalists "came to America to enjoy greater liberty of conscience than they could obtain in England. They had certainly set their hearts on it; at least the principal men and the ministers had done so; for they no sooner obtained in America that liberty of conscience which they sought than they endeavoured to monopolize it all to themselves; and with their good will would not suffer a neighbor to have an atom of it" (in Smylie, 1971: 127). The Episcopalians clung tenaciously to the belief that they were the true Church, being persecuted as opponents of godly order.

Yet, the most significant effect of the "Great Fear" was the prevention of any Anglican bishop being sent to the New World until after American independence had been achieved. The myth caught fire in New England and spread to the Middle Atlantic region, particularly New York City (where there was an Anglican establishment), and to Philadelphia. It warmed the hearts of fellow-dissenters in England to guarantee that although the American missionaries of the Church of England might propose one plan after another for settling "purely ecclesiastical" bishops, all such attempts were frustrated. The failure of the Laudian project resulted in the failure of any regular episcopal jurisdiction in the American colonies for 150 years (see Wright, 1962: 72-97).

Pseudo-Restoration: Lineage Not Monopoly

In a sense the restoration of Charles II to the English throne was a foregone conclusion from the start of the Rebellion. The English insistence upon fidelity to "tradition" made it difficult to conceive of a revolutionary government ever bringing order and stability to such a society. The failure of the Westminster Assembly to find a national religion, the martial quality of Cromwell's ascent and control, and the presence of an active and amiable Stuart monarch in Holland all served to insure the end of the Protectorate (see Bosher, 1951: 6-12; Cragg, 1966). Charles wished to return England to the traditions of her fathers and to her mother church. By the end of his reign he had created a religio-social situation giving fixity to the lines of denominational division and paving the way for the realization of the pluralistic structure foreshadowed during the Protectorate.

Before he departed Holland for England, Charles issued the Declaration of Breda, a general declaration of amnesty for all except the regicides. He stated, in part, "Because the passion and uncharitableness of the times have produced several opinions in religion, by which men are engaged in parties and animosities against each other . . . we do declare a liberty to tender consciences and that no man shall be disquieted or called in question for differences of opinion in matters of religion which do not disturb the peace of the kingdom" (in Bryant, 1968:

84-85).[17] However, Charles chose his words with discretion. He acknowledged neither "sects" nor "denominations" but *opinions* and *parties,* which in his monopolistically-oriented mind were all a part and would all remain a part of the one Church of England. Influenced heavily by a well-organized Laudian party, Charles had not kept abreast of either religious or social changes occurring in England during his exile. The organization and maneuverings of this small but highly effective "sectarian" group is of significance not only because of its influence on Charles' conception of the religious situation in England, but also because in terms of the model it provides an illustration of an entrenched sect-like "fifth column" (during the Protectorate) as a religious expression of royalist sympathies and Restoration politics (see Underdown, 1960; Davies, 1955; Bosher, 1951).

The King moved quickly in reinstituting the Anglican establishment. Episcopalians were restored to important posts, and Puritan clergy were ejected. The court acted singularly on the Jacobean principle of "No Bishop, no King" by insisting upon the reestablishment of the Church of England along traditional episcopal lines.[18] The Restoration Parliament was composed of Laudian schooled churchmen who supported the King in his endeavors. The Puritans were naturally disturbed by these events and made concerted attempts to get Charles to heed their requests. The Presbyterians who had supported the Restoration felt particularly cheated (see Abernathy, 1965; Lamont, 1963). Charles' answer to them came at the Savoy Conference of 1661, when the Puritans were given opportunity to state their grievances to the Anglican bishops they had earlier deprived — hardly an impartial body!

The list of grievances presented by Richard Baxter to the bishops contained many points upon which they were willing to yield. However, it became readily apparent that the Puritans were asking for much more than minor modifications. They wanted abolition of a required liturgy and changes in doctrines that the bishops considered essential to the maintenance of the historic plausibility structure of the Church of England. The bishops "took up a strong and unyielding position behind primitive custom and Catholic usage" (Proctor & Frere, 1965: 189), refusing the Puritan objections. A new Prayer Book (1662) was introduced as part of an Act of Uniformity under which failure to use this service book for all public worship led to clerical deprivation and ejection. All clergy and schoolmasters were also required to declare that they believed it unlawful to take up arms against the King and that the Scottish Solemn League and Covenant was an unlawful oath. Denouncing the credo of northern Presbyterianism and insisting upon rigid conformity to the rites of the Restoration Book, Charles' government was arguing that what was wrong with the Protectorate in government was also wrong in religion. In order to have a healthy nation, it was necessary to have both king and bishop. Church and state must once again be welded into an unbreakable whole in order for the nation to prosper. People wanting the monarchy restored had to be prepared to submit to episcopacy as well. Thus Dr. Robert South, preaching at the consecration of a new bishop in 1661 proclaimed, "The Church of England glories in *nothing more* than that she is the truest friend to kings and kingly government, of any other church in the world; that they were the same hands that took the crown from the King's head and the mitre from the bishops" (in Bennett, 1969: 155, italics mine).

The new government, strongly influenced by the prelates who under the Protectorate had been the schoolmasters and teachers of members of the Restoration Parliament and court, acted quickly against all opposition. A repetition of the debacle of the twenty years immediately past would not be allowed to occur. A weak and fractionated England would be too easy a mark for her enemies. It was apparent, too, that while they may have represented something else, the disputes, bickerings, and hostilities of the time were expressed in terms of religion. If the nation were to be one, then the church must also be one. Those who refused to accept the discipline of the Church could not expect the privileges of citizenship. "A clear line therefore was to be drawn between conformists and non-conformists, and the latter must be penalized and controled" (Moorman, 1963: 252).[19] Here, however, within what sound in terms of the model like highly church-like statements, the faults in the monopolistic establishment that Charles was trying to recreate were showing. The tacit admission that the Church of England could not comprehend the entirety of the populace of the state signals the fact that while the Stuart lineage might be restored, the Church of England monopoly that had existed under Charles I and his predecessors would not rise again. Charles II would have to settle for a "church" that in typological terms would never have the characteristics that would make it the same as the earlier structure. The Restoration "church" was an established sect. "The resurgent Laudianism of the Restoration was a creed shorn of the political and economic aims by which Laud had alienated the propertied classes, and the new alliance of parson and squire was cemented by the Church's surrender of any pretension to political independence" (Bosher, 1951: 2).

The ecclesio-political situation creating this state of affairs was facilitated by a series of acts of Parliament subsequently known as the Clarendon Code, named for Edward Hyde, Earl of Clarendon, Lord Chancellor, Charles' chief minister and architect of the Restoration settlement. It consisted of (1) the Corporation Act of 1661, which was essentially similar to the aforementioned (2) Act of Uniformity of 1662. It required those holding civic office to renounce the Solemn League and Covenant, to swear not to take up arms against the King, and to be communicants of the Church of England. (3) The Conventicle Act of 1664 was even more important to the growing sectarianism of the Protectorate. This Act made it illegal for anyone over sixteen years old to attend any "assembly, conventicle, or meeting under colour or pretence of any exercise of religion, in other manner than according to the liturgy and practice of the Church of England." In 1666 (4) the Five Mile Act was issued, forbidding any non-conformist minister from living or visiting within five miles of any place in which he had previously resided and served. It was this series of acts which effectively divided England between conformists and non-conformists (see Moorman, 1963: 252-253). "After this failure of mutual adjustment and understanding [on the part of the Presbyterians and the Episcopalians], it must be recognized that the Church of England was no longer the Church of all the English people" (Parsons & Jones, 1937: 44). It is thus in the Clarendon Code as much as the earlier Protectorate sectarianism that one finds the beginnings of denominationalism in England, "the transformation of Puritanism into Dissent" (Lacey, 1969: 15).[20]

One final act of Charles' reign that concerns us is the Test Act of 1673. It required that all those holding civil or military offices were to receive the Holy Communion in accordance with the rites of the Church of England, to denounce the Romish doctrine of transubstantiation, and to take the oaths of supremacy and allegiance. This act was directed more towards the Roman Catholics, who were then sweeping the country, and in whose arms Charles died.[21] However, it also offended the Puritans. Ironically, its final outcome was to insult the Anglican altar, for it became thereby an instrument of Parliament used for purely perfunctory purposes of state (see Neill, 1965: 180-181; Harvey, 1971: 156-169). Yet here denominationalism had its first wedge. No longer was it argued that all men of England could be incorporated into one Church. The monopoly was broken with the severing of the head of Charles I. Although his son made a sincere effort to restore the Church of England to its "church-like" position, the most he could accomplish was a movement from the entrenched sect type to the established sect. A fully developed Anglican *theological* position - hereafter referred to as "normative Anglicanism" — was molded by the Laudians and compacted into final form during the years when "prelacy" was outlawed by the Protectorate (see McAdoo, 1965; More & Cross, 1951). This "Caroline" position returned from exile with Charles II, but like the monarch himself, it was more a showpiece of English traditionalism than an instrument for total systemic reconstruction (see Bosher, 1951: 278-283).

Thus, incipient denominationalism marks the end of Charles II's reign. Like all denominationalism, its roots lie in the outward politico-economic structuring of its sociocultural environment (see C. Hill, 1969: 192-197, 205-210). The Clarendon Code, although intended to put a stop to the rise of Puritan sectaries, in fact had the opposite effect. It acknowledged for the first time *formally,* in law, that the people inhabiting England could no longer all be united into the same religious institution. It also acknowledged that the Church of England was to be something other than a "church" in church-sect terms. The seeds were planted for denominationalism. Monopolism was yielding to pluralism. It is only after the abdication of James II, Charles' successor, and the Glorious Revolution that followed, that the full implications of the untraversable gulf created by the Clarendon Code become fully visible (see Howard, 1975).[22]

Into Denominationalism

Monopolism as a governing principle for English society died with Charles I in 1649. It took about forty years more, however, for pluralism to be enthroned "over his dead body" in the persons of William and Mary, who reigned as co-regents and constitutional monarchs.[23] Their reign was the result of the various processes that had been working in England since the late sixteenth century and formally signaled the end of monopolism as a social base for English society. Pluralism was certainly Charles I's deepest foe. While addressing the problem in terms of the theological questions of the time, both Charles and Laud understood the latent pluralistic tendencies of Puritanism as the real "sin" to be purged from Englishmen's lives. Despite the important events to occur in the reigns of the monarchs who followed the co-regents, from 1689 to 1702 was a crucial period for the future development of both English ecclesiastical politics and religious life in the American colonies (see Lovejoy, 1972). F.G. James comments on the persistence of the religious variable: "If one wishes to give priority to a single thread in the Stuart drama, that of religion might offer the best explanation of events . . . After 1688 the most consistent differences between Whigs and Tories were religious in nature. Viewed from such an angle the central constitutional struggle of the era itself, that between Crown and Parliament, appears as a battle for control of the Church" (1970: 229).

Two events are of particular importance to an analysis of the religious situa-
tions in England and the colonies during this period. These are the passing of the
Toleration Act, and the separation of a number of bishops and priests from the
Church of England following the Glorious Revolution — the Nonjuror Schism.

The Toleration Act

William of Orange was a Dutch Calvinist who knew well that large numbers
of Englishmen (first the Puritans, then the Anglicans) had come to the Low Countries seeking refuge from persecution. His country tolerated a great deal of Protestant pluralism, something the English simultaneously welcomed and derided
(see Miller, 1970: 102-118). Mary, his wife, was an Anglican by birth and outward
profession, but she had lived with her husband in a strongly Protestant country
and never censured the general toleration there. William's particular interest in
religion is difficult to identify. For example, he was willing to see the missionary
efforts of the Church of England in the colonies continue and gave some measure
of support to them. Certainly his actions show no deep-seated animus toward the
established church or its hierarchy (see Bennett, 1966). On the other hand, his
sympathies undoubtedly lay with the Protestant cause within the realm of
England. Despite the fact that it was necessary for him to conform outwardly to
the Church of England, William nevertheless found it difficult to see his Protestant brethren suffering under the conditions imposed by the Clarendon Code (see
Hutton, 1913: 245-254). Furthermore, many members of Parliament held the
dissenters' ideology in high esteem. While there was a fairly equal division between High and Low Churchmen in the House of Lords, Commons was strongly
Whig and aligned against the normative Anglicans.

Although all members of Parliament had to show outward allegiance to the
establishment, the dominating theological influence emanating from William's
hierarchy was that of the latitudinarians. This group, from whom the current
designation "broad church" originates, was a strong force in the Revolutionary
English Church. They professed a moralistically-oriented, non-dogmatic
theology, a disdain for ceremony, and a loose and comprehensive doctrine of the
Church, resulting in a liberal attitude toward those who could not accept the more
obviously Catholic doctrines of the Caroline divines (see Cragg, 1950: 61ff., 199;
Moorman, 1963: 255-257). In terms of the model, the latitudinarians were much
more anxious to see the Church of England regain its place as the monopolistic
church than maintain its status as a favored established sect. Thus, they were
more than willing to make numerous concessions to the Dissenters in exchange
for their allegiance to the Establishment. In 1689 the latitudinarians framed a plan
for the reconstruction of a comprehensive Protestant church. It failed to win acceptance because of the relatively weak numerical strength of the latitudinarians
among the rank-and-file clergy. Although the bishops of the upper house of the
bicameral Convocation were quite solidly latitudinarian, the necessity of agreement among the two houses defeated the plan. Convocations were prorogued by
Royal Writ in 1717, however, striking a major blow to the Laudian party in England
and retarding American appeals for a bishop (see Meza, 1973; Switzer, 1932). What
latitudinarianism ultimately provided, then, was a theological rationale for the
"class churches" or denominations that developed in eighteenth century
England.

In Parliament, however, the Dissenters had a better time of it. Although the
Clarendon Code attempted to stamp out dissent, by an ironic quirk it became one

of the first expressions of its legitimation and institutionalization. It recognized with great seriousness that dissent existed, that this dissent was widespread enough to be organized, and that it could not be incorporated into the structure of the Church of England. The new Parliament of William and Mary, faced with strong pressures from both the latitudinarians and the dissenters, was not likely to permit a policy as stringent as this to persist. It therefore passed the Toleration Act (see J.R. Jones, 1972: 98-167). Though this act did not remove the civil disabilities upon Dissenters generally, nor *any* of the prohibitions toward Roman Catholics or Unitarians, it did allow those Protestants who professed their loyalty to the monarchy the privilege to meet in their own places of worship. However, they could do so only with the doors unlocked, and the bishop of the diocese in which they were located had to be given notice of their existence. Dissenting ministers also might be licensed, if they accepted (additionally) the Thirty-Nine Articles, save those on infant baptism.

To the twentieth-century mind, this Act may show little pluralistic religious liberty. The restrictions on participation in political life, for example, remained, but they were no longer the whip they had been when coupled with the refusal of meeting-house privileges. It was now possible for a person to receive Communion from the established church consistent with the requirements of the Test Act, and yet attend and take part in the Dissenters' meetings. Most Dissenters could do this without considerable qualms of conscience. Their theology was receptionist, the Holy Communion was only "real" when the believer believed it to be so. Only normative Anglicans with an "objective" doctrine of Real Presence would find this practice repugnant. Over twenty years passed before any attempt was made by the monarchy to correct the abuses of this situation, when the Occasional Conformity Act was passed by Queen Anne's Tory Parliament in 1711. This attempt to alleviate the misuse of Test Act privileges by Dissenters, however, was repealed by the Whigs in 1718 and was never reinstated (see Moorman, 1963: 271-272). It was thus only a seven-year interlude on what was otherwise a clearly linear path over the next century and a half.

For the common Englishman it was now clear that there was to be no single "church" of England. Anglicanism was only one theological alternative among many, albeit one blessed by the state. Nonconformity was well on its way toward complete legitimation. Pluralism and denominationalism in its wake, had quietly triumphed. Whatever the religion of England was to become, it would clearly not be classical normative Anglicanism. That the Established Church could continue to maintain its earlier strength and hold over the people also became less and less true. In the context of the model, then, although the Church of England would retain, even up to the present, an aura of churchliness, it was no longer to do so in the presence of isolated and secretive entrenched sects, but before the threat of dynamic sects and thence thriving denominations. Despite its own technical establishment, the Church of England itself continued to become more and more denominational in character.

The Nonjurors

Not only were William and Mary questionable in the eyes of High Churchmen for their continental Protestant affinities, but some also suspected their right to reign at all. This led to the Nonjuror controversy. James II, Mary's father and William's uncle, fled from England while William and Mary were entering, but he did not abdicate the throne. Parliament, however, was quick to act, declaring the

FIGURE 3

THE PROCESSES OF RELIGIO-SOCIAL CHANGE IN ENGLAND: I

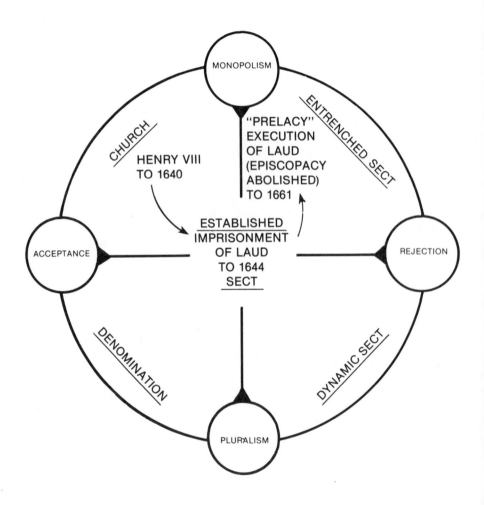

FIGURE 4

THE PROCESSES OF RELIGIO-SOCIAL CHANGE IN ENGLAND: II

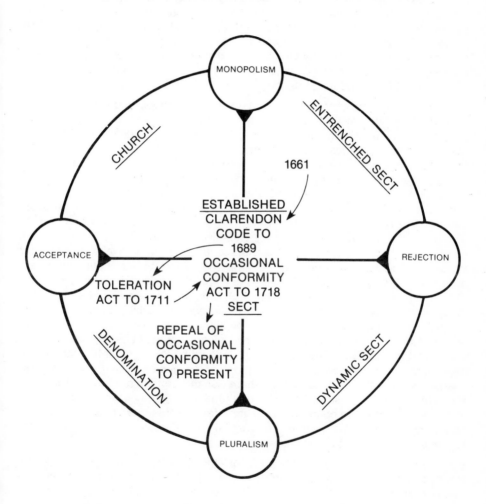

throne vacant, and offering it jointly to the couple as constitutional monarchs (at Mary's insistence). Politically it was a sensible and workable arrangement. Ecclesiastically, however, it was to raise questions in the minds of many clerics.

Two doctrines pervaded Anglican theology at the time with respect to the nature of government. One was that of Divine Right. The King ruled by the direct authority of God mediated to him by the unction he received at his coronation by the Archbishop of Canterbury. Due to the veneration of Charles I following his martyrdom, and the subsequent influence of the Laudians at the Restoration, the theological doctrine of Divine Right did not die with him (see Bosher, 1951; Legg, 1964: 690-702). The other dogmatic concept was that the King's subjects owed him "Passive Obedience." That is, they were to obey and be loyal to him as long as he lived. This doctrine was particularly strong in the Laudian party and tended to weld this brand of churchmanship to the Stuart succession. One writer of the period recalls, "I may be positive where I heard one sermon of repentance, faith, and the renewing of the Holy Ghost, I heard three of the other [on passive obedience]; and 'tis hard to say whether Jesus Christ or King Charles the First were oftener mentioned and magnified" (in Macaulay, 1967: II 401).

A sizeable group of churchmen had reservations about their loyalty to James. Most of these were willing to accept the Parliamentary arrangement in spite of possible deficiencies. Straka (1962: ix) states the case of those who approved of the co-regents' ascendancy: "From the view of the Revolution Anglican, the Revolution was not a departure, but a restoration of true divine right Protestant monarchy and a return to the national unity of Elizabeth's days." A few clerics, including the Archbishop of Canterbury, were unable to bring their consciences to this point. To them the action of Parliament was not merely a disgrace but a sin. James was the only rightful ruler of England, and neither Parliament nor anyone else on earth could deprive him of his God-given authority.[24] Yet the new Parliament required that all clergy subscribe to the standard loyalty oath toward William and Mary. The Nonjurors refused. They were therefore suspended and after the canonical six months' period had elapsed, deprived. But the problem for the Church still was not solved. Often high officials, these clerics had to be formally tried in order to be removed from their positions. Like their monarch, they had not abdicated. This, in turn, raised the serious question of the authority that lay behind their deprivation. By canon law a bishop could not be deprived unless a serious crime, either ecclesiastical or civil, could be laid against him, and in any case deprivation was to be the judgment of an *ecclesiastical* court. Yet, no charges were forthcoming. Likewise, there was difficulty in determining who had the authority to fill these vacancies. For a time the benefices were allowed to remain vacant, but these posts were too important for this to continue indefinitely. Latitudinarians eventually were found to fill all the places, but with the unfortunate result of a "rent in the seamless robe of Christ."

As in any schism the question arose: Who were the schismatics? From the standpoint of English church history as a whole, they were the Nonjurors. This was not, of course, the Nonjurors' self-conception. Rather, they saw themselves as the true Church of England, disclaimed all responsibility for what had occurred, and placed all of the blame upon those who had consented to the decision of Parliament. The schism, however, was not a necessary or logical outcome. Episcopacy had been disallowed once before during the Protectorate, and for the most part, the churchmen who were loyal to the Anglican position accepted their fate quietly. They simply worked behind the scenes to produce a favorable outcome at the eventual Restoration. Bosher (1951), for example, notes that many of the Anglican clergy conformed to the Protectorate establishment, and after the ardor of the revolutionary spirit had mellowed, returned to the Prayer Book service. Indeed, Jeremy Taylor, and probably many other less generally well-known priests, is said to have committed the bulk of the Book to memory. The Nonjurors, however, saw Parliament's attempt to dictate religion as a much more serious offence. From their point of view the entire question of the prerogatives of the church with respect to the state *re* the monarchy was in serious jeopardy of being answered wrongly. Parliament had first been so presumptuous as to remove God's Anointed from the throne and to crown another as the lawful monarch. It was now going even further in determining the propriety of filling vacant cures without the legitimating sanctions of the ecclesiastical hierarchy. It was one thing to say, as had Cromwell, that Episcopalians could not worship as they wished. Cromwell's government was, after all, "illegitimate." But it was quite another thing to have the "legitimate" lay government, lacking the crowned monarch's holy anointing and Divine Right, tell the bishops how to do their housekeeping. Pluralism and secularism were creeping into the bishops' chairs , and the Nonjurors would not let it go unnoticed.

To the Nonjurors this extension of Erastianism in Parliament represented a great crime. The Church of England "lost all claim to be considered a true church". Only the Nonjurors could be regarded as the legitimate representatives of the true, catholic, and apostolic succession and Church in England (see Moorman, 1963: 264-265).[25] From this time forth the English Nonjurors became a ritualistic entrenched sect. Their greatest interest was experimentation in forms of liturgical practice and the externals of worship (see B. Wilson, 1966; Anson, 1964). They continued the succession with the help of the Scottish bishops (also Nonjurors) until 1805, when for all practical purposes the movement ceased.

The episcopate in Scotland was never a successful venture, but in connection with the Nonjuror controversy, it deserves some serious attention. There were two attempts to enforce episcopacy in Scotland after the Knoxian reformation. The first, on which Laud capitalized for his liturgical endeavors, was inaugurated by James I in 1610. The second occurred at the Restoration in 1662. In spite of all efforts on the part of the English, whether vigorously militant or politely conciliatory, the Scots would not accept episcopacy (see W.R. Foster, 1958). Moreover, with its intimate connection to the Stuarts (the only aid to its maintenance), the never-genuinely-established episcopate in Scotland was not about to take the oath of allegiance to the co-regents. Thus from the time of William and Mary to the present, the Church of Scotland has been officially and unquestionably Presbyterian:

> . . . and Episcopalians became a brutally persecuted minority. After the rebellion of 1745, matters were even worse; the penal laws were so severe that it was not possible for an episcopal priest to minister at one time to more than five persons . . . And yet, through all these bitter years, the Scottish [Episcopal] Church kept itself in being, and maintained not merely the episcopal succession, but also its own liturgical tradition, and a strong consciousness of its own independent existence [Neill, 1965: 279-280].

Toleration toward Episcopalianism in Scotland was to increase just as toward

Nonconformity in England. But it was slow in coming. The denominationalism that arose in England as a result of the Toleration Act did not rise as quickly in Scotland, in part because the Scottish Episcopalians did not adopt the same attitude toward themselves as did the dissenters in England. There, as the eighteenth century wore on, the sectarian militancy of the Jacobean Puritans disappeared into a surrender to the sociocultural system of the Restoration settlement. *"Dissent* still carries the sound of resistance to Apollyon and the Whore of Babylon. *Nonconformity* is self-effacing and apologetic: it asks to be left alone" (E.P. Thompson, 1963: 350). To the Scottish Episcopalians, on the other hand, with their love and deep appreciation of rite and ceremony, there was but one true Church, and that was the Church Catholic, of which episcopacy was an indubitable mark (see Goldie, 1951: 32-62).

Merely to dismiss the Nonjurors, both English and Scottish, as a group of misguided High Churchmen or eccentric royalists is to commit a serious sociological error. The Nonjurors represent a manner of thinking and acting, descending primarily from Laudian resistance during the Protectorate, that is an important element in understanding Episcopalianism in both the British Isles and the United States. This viewpoint we may term "exclusivism" and mark by its anti-denominationalism. It is the sectarian element in Anglicanism that stands over against the much more frequently noted Anglican comprehensiveness. In the church-sect sense, it is a two edged-sword. It militates for churchliness. However, when this status is not forthcoming it moves more or less strongly, depending upon the historical circumstances and the relative strength of the other bodies with which it must contend, toward sectarianism. This is the logical converse of Little's (1969: 76, 129) assertions about the characteristics of Puritanism that are likely to be manifest under particular historical circumstances. Little, of course, gives himself more to charting and explaining the "rise" or Puritanism than the "fall" of Anglicanism. Perhaps because it, indeed, represents the "losing" side of Anglicanism, this sectarian aspect has been given less attention. One of the functions of an analysis such as this is to bring these alternative postures to light and demonstrate their connection to both internal and external variables. As a *church,* exclusivism fit Anglicanism. As a *denomination,* it did not, and a change was necessary. For those who would not make this belief-system alteration, the *sectarian* action-system provided a viable outlet. This happened only because of certain specifiable changes in the larger sociocultural system that interacted with *already established* belief and action structures in the religious organization.

There was thus nothing in the theology of the Nonjurors that could enable them to become a denomination alongside the Church of England. As the reign of William and Mary signaled the end of monopolism as a social base for English society, the Nonjuring succession began a new religio-cultural form for Anglicanism. This occurrence resulted in the existence of Anglican bishops who were nevertheless not "Church of England." The Church *in* Scotland, while not recognized at that point by the Church of England, became the first effort at organized Anglicanism outside of the royal monopoly. In these critical years, Anglicanism had developed a sectarian theology as well as a denominational establishment. Although the "validity" of the Nonjurors' orders would be questioned by the latitudinarians on political grounds, these churchmen provided the necessary succession for the American Episcopalians and forced British recognition of the principle of religious liberty. It remained for the Americans to effect a synthesis between latitudinarianism and Nonjuror theology.

This fifty-year span of English history produced the realization of the pluralistic tendencies latent in the Puritan ideology (see Figures 3 and 4). At the close of this period strong denominational tendencies developed in England and a sectarian Anglicanism to the North. As these two forces met, the "Episcopalians" in America would continue to solidify organizationally within the pluralistic social system that was also well on its way into denominationalism.

Chapter 4
PLURALISTIC SOLIDIFICATION

Looking Backward and Forward

The pluralistic social system and the denominationalism within it were ushered onto the Anglo-American scene by the activities of Parliament and the co-regents at the end of the seventeenth century. Although it would take about a hundred years for the implications of this "event" to be recognized and legitimated, the beginning point is clearly here. The key transitional events include the imprisonment of Laud, the abolition of episcopacy and the eventual decollation of Charles I, the Clarendon Code, and finally the Glorious Revolution and the toleration it brought. Since the denominational form is still in process, one cannot follow it to its end, nor do I intend to give a detailed account of developments up to the present. I would suggest, rather, that by the year 1800 the clear shape of things to come was fairly well delineated. A few occurrences of the nineteenth century help to round out the picture.

In these one hundred years of transition to denominationalism, the American scene is very important and thus the focal point in this phase of our study. Nevertheless, one of the bubbles of our historiography that we must burst is the idea that the American colonials and the British at home had no contact. Some of the emigrants had a tremendous and continuing correspondence with those who remained in England, and this interaction must not be forgotten in spite of our concentration here upon the American side of the story.

In England, Queen Anne was the last of the High Church monarchs to govern. She hoped to return her kingdom to the conditions of the reign of Charles II, if not the earlier Stuarts. Toward this end, she attempted the revival of beatific religio-political ceremonies and stressed court pomp. Nevertheless, Anne found herself constantly subject to the checks of a Parliament divided between two major "parties" — Tories and Whigs, whose composition in turn reflected a religious base.[1] When the Tories were in power, the Queen got what she wanted. When the Whigs held the reins, she lost. During the Tory period, the Occasional Conformity Act was passed. In terms of the model it pushed the Church of England back into the established sect category, temporarily threatening the sects of Dissenters, which had become "established" and protodenominational during the co-regency. After seven years' duration a return to Whig policies brought the repeal of this Act.

The one lasting benefit of this reign was Queen Anne's Bounty, revenues for the Church claimed by Henry VIII at his reformation and given by Anne to augment the salaries of underpaid Church of England clergy (see Brown, 1968; Best, 1964; C. Hill, 1969: 41, 214-215). Other than this, Anne's efforts to restore the royal

FIGURE 5

THE PROCESSES OF RELIGIO-SOCIAL CHANGE IN NEW ENGLAND

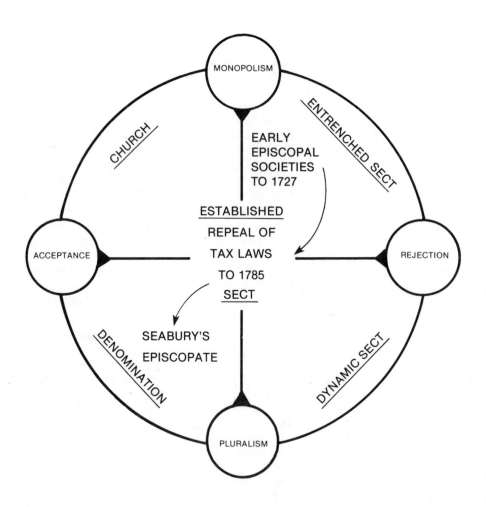

monopoly were futile. Her total dependence upon Parliament's grace to achieve her desires shows that English society had changed, and that monopolism would no longer be a viable principle for social organization. Anne's feeble steps backward, more than anything else, are evidence for the great strides forward of the Glorious Revolution. It was not a royal monopoly Anne exercised but the will of a Parliamentary party whose own ideas and ambitions brought them into a natural alliance with this monarch. From this point in English history, the disposition of the Crown is much less relevant in determining policy than the disposition of Parliament and the interests it represents. "The proverbial phrase 'Queen Anne is dead,' came to mean that something had disappeared finally and irrevocably. If the age of faith ever existed, it was over by 1714" (C. Hill, 1966: 312).[2]

Missionary Monopolism: The Venerable Society

On June 16, 1701, Thomas Bray, D.D., sometime commissary for the Church in Maryland, and also active in the chartering of the colony of Georgia, was granted a charter to erect the Society for the Propagation of the Gospel in Foreign Parts (see the *Classified Digest,* 1893: 1-87; 743-757, 849-856, also Rice, 1961: 45-65). "Through its missionaries, who reported to London once a year, and lay members in the colonies, and through the sermons preached annually before the lay and clerical members at the parish church of St. Mary-le-Bow, through the publication of tracts and press notices, and through intimate connections with the hierarchy, the S.P.G. quickly became the central agency for the propagation of the Church of England as well as of the gospel in America. It represented British imperialism in ecclesiastical guise" (Bridenbaugh, 1962: 57). The Venerable Society was to be the focal point for American religio-political controversy for the next seventy-five years. Unlike Bray's earlier Society for Promoting Christian Knowledge (S.P.C.K.) founded in 1689, the S.P.G. was not simply a voluntary association of well-disposed individuals. Rather, as a result of the petition for charter granted by William III, it was "a regularly incorporated and chartered society, with the support and authorization of both Church and State" (Neill, 1965: 197-198). Bray justified this status on the basis that there were many people willing to contribute financially to the cause of the Church in the colonies, if there were a duly constituted body to supervise these affairs.

The charter granted by the King was a generous one, sufficiently vague to allow a great latitude of interpretation. This latitude probably accounts for William, the Dutch Calvinist, signing the charter. It may also explain the later problems that beset and maligned the Society. The charter referred to "the Instruction of Our People in the Christian Religion," "a sufficient Maintenance . . . for an Orthodox Clergy to live amongst them," and "Provision . . . as may be necessary for the Propagation of the Gospel in those Parts" (see Herklots, 1966: 51-52). Difficulties arose because these phrases were subject to differing interpretations by the Laudian Anglicans who formed the majority of the S.P.G. members and missionaries on the one side, and the Dissenters or Nonconformists on the other. The Church of England missionaries were to take the words in their most narrow sense: "The Christian Religion" was Anglicanism. "An Orthodox Clergy" were Anglican priests. "The Propagation of the Gospel" was bringing Dissenters back into the Anglican fold.

Above all, the only way these ends could possibly be fully and finally accomplished was by the consecration of resident bishops to rule the colonial Church.

... No sooner was the Society established on a firm foundation than it began to direct its efforts toward substituting a control by bishops resident in the colonies for the jurisdiction of the Bishop of London. However innocent this intention may have been, the Anglican Episcopal organization was too closely interwoven with the English governmental system to make it possible to keep the matter within the spiritual field. Moreover, the Independent congregations in America knew the Church of England bishop only as an oppressive tyrant, backed by the strong arm of civil power. For these reasons, the attempt of the Society to secure an American episcopate involved not only itself but the whole colonial church in a series of political contests, the outcome of which marked the first great crisis in American history [A.L. Cross, 1964: 36].

In short, as far as American religious history during its first one hundred years is concerned, the Venerable Society was perhaps the most important religious society ever founded. The wrath the Society received for its efforts toward establishing a resident episcopate was due primarily to the anti-episcopal myth that had been increasing its "objective" status ever since the Laudian attempt at creating a bishop for New England in 1638. Thus, Carroll (1970: xv) notes, "Like any ideological predisposition, religion impelled men to interpret their experiences according to a predetermined scheme — in this case, a plot to destroy colonial liberty. Having articulated such statements, the American [Puritan] clergy became enmeshed in its own rhetoric and thereafter created a world of reality which probably never existed."

The myth had only been helped to grow by the few other attempts to provide for an American episcopate before the founding of the S.P.G. The first of these instances occurred around 1664 when the "Chamber at Amsterdam" wrote to the governor and council of New Netherlands that it had received word from England that Charles II, "being inclined to reduce all his kingdoms under one form of government in Church and State, hath taken care that Commissioners are ready in England to repair to New England to install Bishops there . . . ." If this were true, the English authorities soon had a change of heart. "For in the set of private instructions issued to the commissioners, they ordered them to take no steps in the direction of substituting episcopacy for the existing form of religion" (A.L. Cross, 1964: 91). Whether, then, this was an actual attempt to establish an American episcopate or simply a rumor, it nevertheless is a worthwhile illustration of the way people were *thinking* with respect to the Anglican episcopate. It was a matter of the government of the people, of political rule and the legitimation of power. This was the classical Protestant argument against the extension of the Anglican system. Bishops were retained in England at the Reformation not because they were of the *essence* of Christianity but for political reasons. Indeed, there had been tremendous vacillation on the part of Anglicans in regard to the question of the institution of the episcopate previous to the Laudian synthesis, and it appeared again in the latitudinarians (see New, 1964: 55-58; Mason, 1914: 1-22 ff.). If one held that bishops were not of divine institution but rather for purposes of government (as virtually all other Protestants did), then the Anglicans in the colonies obviously had no need of bishops for "spiritual" reasons. They wanted them to gain political domination and, eventually, wealth. No matter how much the S.P.G. missionaries might protest that they were asking for bishops with only spiritual powers, the "political bishop" could not be erased from the Protestant mind.

A later attempt to provide a bishop was made by Lord Chancellor Clarendon in a proposal to send Dr. Alexander Murray to Virginia. Murray had been a traveling companion of the Restoration monarch, and the plan was approved by the King-in-Council, with letters patent for its execution. Nevertheless, this, too, came to naught, probably because of the change-over from the Clarendon to Cabal ministries. Note once again the close tie of ecclesiastical to civil matters. Bishops were considered agents of the state, "in the nature of an ecclesiastical sheriff," said English Chief Justice Francis North, with their appointment conditioned by the political affairs of the times much more than by any "spiritual" reasons. The question, apparently, is not, "Was it so?" but, "Did it have to be so?" Could Episcopalianism flourish, even survive, outside of a church-like setting? What would the Scottish case prove?

The final of these pre-S.P.G. efforts simply added more fire to the arguments of the Dissenters. In 1695 Chaplain John Miller in New York, by then a royal colony, proposed that a bishop be sent to the province as its only governor, with both civil and ecclesiastical administration as his cure. The bishop would be a suffragan to the London See and be responsible to the incumbent there. This is, of course, precisely what the Puritans feared and prophesied as the outcome of any American episcopate, whether it was stated as frankly as Miller's proposal or in the "spiritual" phrases of the Venerable Society (see A.L. Cross, 1964: 88-112).

The S.P.G. met for the first time after its chartering on June 27, 1701. Bray had already begun to agitate on the subject of an American episcopate previous to the official establishing of the Society, and was now anxious that this work be continued. The Reverend George Kieth was appointed a traveling missionary to discover the best points for the inauguration of the Church's work. Upon arriving at Boston in 1702, he encouraged the Reverend John Talbot, chaplain of the boat on which they had come to the New World, to go with him. The pair spent most of the next two years traveling from Boston to the Carolinas preaching, making converts, and beginning new churches. Kieth then returned to England, leaving his companion in New Jersey. From 1702 onward Talbot would be a lonely but constant agitator in the Society for the American episcopate.

> The poor Church has nobody upon the spot to comfort or confirm her children; nobody to ordain several that are willing to serve, were they authorized, for the work of the Ministry. Therefore they fall back again into the herd of Dissenters, rather than they will be at the Hazard and Charge to goe as far as England for orders: so that we have seen several Counties, Islands, and Provinces, which have hardly an orthodox minister am'st them, which might have been supply'd, had we been so happy as to see a Bishop or Suffragan Apud Americanos [in A.L. Cross, 1964: 93].

Talbot's request concerns only the spiritual function of the episcopate, and he indicates elsewhere that the bishop would receive his living from a tithe paid by all the Anglican clergy and not from taxation. In 1705, however, fourteen clergy assembled in Burlington, New Jersey, and sent the archbishops and bishops a petition stating their needs. These included not only the spiritual ministrations of Talbot's letters, but also contemplated an establishment likely to arouse opposition among the Dissenters. Two years later, after Talbot had gone to England and received some encouragement, the Reverend Evan Evans, the first S.P.G. missionary in Philadelphia, introduced some new points in his appeal to the Society.

First, not only is a bishop needed to ordain clergy but also to keep order among them in such disputes as might, and often did, arise. Furthermore, a bishop would enable the clergy to have more power in the governing of their congregations. "Without the aid of episcopal sanction," Evans claimed, the clergy were powerless to denounce "the leaders among their people . . . even in cases of the grossest irregularities of living." What Evans was asking for were "spiritual courts" virtually identical to those in England, one of the prime targets of the Dissenters' venom.

Perhaps in direct response to these petitions, the Bishop of London set forth some "Observations" regarding a suffragan for the colonies. This bishop would provide the necessary element of episcopal orders for confirmations and ordinations but would otherwise function with no greater powers than those presently allowed commissaries, i.e. without "jurisdiction." Nothing ever resulted directly from these proposals (see A.L. Cross, 1964: 95-96, 277-278). We note developing in this early denominational period in England, however, an attitude toward bishops as purely ecclesiastical functionaries that further coroborates our assessment of the ecclesiastical situation there. The first inklings among ecclesiastical officialdom of the separation of church and state, a critically important move for pluralism, were beginning to appear.

In 1709, and again in 1713, petitions were directed to Queen Anne herself for an American suffragan. The earlier memorial, while appealing primarily to Anne's religious interest and devotion, nevertheless begged "leave to add that we are informed that the French received several great advantages from their establishing a [Roman Catholic] Bishop at Quebec" (see Albright, 1964: 97-98). The response to this petition was the issuing of a Royal Letter in 1711 to provide further funds for the work of the Society (see Brown, 1968: 331-332). The second request, originating from New England, never actually reached the Queen (see A.L. Cross, 1964: 98-99), but numerous similar memorials were being directed to the Society to give it sufficient grounds to petition again. This time, probably as a result of the work of Francis Nicholson (see Winton, 1948), the Queen was willing to take up the matter in earnest and ordered a bill, based upon a plan framed by a Society committee, prepared for Parliament. Anne died in 1714, with the Act yet to be considered. In America, however, a "seat for a bishop" had been purchased by Governor Robert Hunter of New York, and he had been ordered by the Society to prepare for the episcopal arrival. Hunter had been attempting to secure this appointment for his friend Jonathan Swift, Dean of St. Patrick's, Dublin, and author of many works, including *Gulliver's Travels*. In the meantime, Talbot had purchased a house in Burlington for the bishop on behalf of the Society and Hunter, its agent, and he, too, received orders that it be prepared for habitation (see A.L. Cross, 1964: 93-94; Burr, 1954: 336-372). This was the closest the colonies ever came to having a bishop in the post-Laudian period.

Dissenting Denominations

In 1690, one year after the assent of William and Mary, an effort was begun to unite the dissenting bodies that comprised the largest numbers of English Nonconformists. All of them wanted greater influence upon the government. In 1691 the "Heads of Agreement" was entered into by a number of outstanding Puritan divines, including Increase Mather. However almost as soon as it came into being, this union was embroiled in theological controversies that led to its virtual collapse by 1694, when the Congregationalist faction withdrew. The ascendancy of Queen Anne and the Tory government forced the Dissenters to reconsider their position. In 1702 the Presbyterians, Baptists, and Congregationalists formed "the body of the Dissenting Ministers of the Three Denominations in and about the City of London" to address the Crown upon matters of concern to the dissenting interest (see Bridenbaugh, 1962: 33-36; B.L. Manning, 1952: 1-7, 19-33).

The use of the term "denomination" here is significant. Although it is undoubtedly more refined in its use as a sociological concept in church-sect theory, the term is taken from everyday use. The sociological use of "denomination" is similar to its everyday use, except that the former is not judgmental. However, it is precisely the judgmental sense of the term that is significant here. By this time, the Dissenters eschewed the term "sect" in favor of "denomination" because of the negative social and political connotations of the former. "Denomination" implies that there is some element of unity or commonality to which all subscribe, even though they call themselves by different names. Thus as Whigs and Tories are both Englishmen, so Presbyterians and Baptists and Congregationalists *and Anglicans* are all English Christians. Official acknowledgment of the Three Denominations, then, would raise obvious questions about the status of the Church of England. How can a "church" remain where pluralistic denominationalism is the working principle for social organization? Normative Anglicanism was forced into a denominational position, even if the "Church of England" remained. The organization of the Three Denominations during Anne's reign is testimony first, to their denominational status previous to her reign; second, to their refusal to see Anglicanism become church-like in the monopolistic sense of that term; and third, to the inability of this monarch to take decisive steps to alter this situation.

The Three Denominations, however, did not achieve the immediate importance that the treatment of it here might suggest. Indeed, aside from formal addresses to the Queen, little was done actively in England until after Anne's death. There was, however, another scene where the Dissenters had an interest: In New England, where they were not dissenters, but the established church. The interaction between these two groups of Englishmen in the new and old countries is given detailed consideration in Bridenbaugh's *Mitre and Sceptre*. One of the outstanding contributions of that book is its recognition of the fact that political intrigue was as much a part of the dissenting interest as were the establishment's maneuverings to Anglicanism. The beginning of this transatlantic association Bridenbaugh places at Increase Mather's participation in the Heads of Agreement in 1691 (see Middlekauf, 1971; Morgan, 1963). While these failed in England, this was not entirely the case in America. In 1705 the Cambridge-Boston Association of Ministers published proposals for the reform of the New England churches and for facilitating communication between local ministerial associations. The proposals were rejected in Massachusetts, but in Connecticut became the Saybrook Platform of Church Discipline (1708). However, the matter did not end there. Over the next three-quarters of a century a prodigious amount of formal and informal correspondence and transoceanic publication issued from the dissenting interests. The content of this material, for all its interest, is far too voluminous to be reported in detail here. However some portions bear rather directly upon our theoretical considerations.

At the outset, two things are worthy of note. One is the person of Benjamin

Colman who, after graduating from Harvard, set out for England in 1695 to spend four years there and make "lasting friendships with Dissenters of every complexion and with many moderate Anglicans as well — connections which would be vital to the Dissenters' cause in later years" (Bridenbaugh, 1962: 35). Colman returned to America but continued his correspondence across the Atlantic. He served as an example to others, both Churchmen and Dissenters, to take up this "educational pastime" and use it to their advantage. One of the Anglican moderates with whom Colman corresponded was White Kennett, then Dean of Peterborough, but soon to be its bishop, and an S.P.G. advocate of the American episcopate. Kennett was not a party man. He was thoroughly repulsed by the high churchmen and yet apparently abhorred the political interests and maneuverings characteristic of the latitudinarian party. He was a man ahead of his time, arguing for the episcopate on the grounds that this was the way Episcopalians chose to organize their religious life. He was perfectly willing to allow other denominations to co-exist with episcopacy as relative equals. In his letters to Colman, Kennett is extremely respectful toward the dissenting interest, putting forth the need for episcopal supervision in the colonies most apologetically on the grounds that more discipline and guidance needs to be provided for those adhering to the "Episcopal Way." He says that the New England churches are "out of our Line, and therefore beyond the Cognizance of any Overseers to be sent from here," and states that the sending of a suffragan to the New England colonies "will not break in upon your national [n.b.] Rites and Customs . . . ." (in A.L. Cross, 1964: 99). In all of this, Kennett is arguing a denominational position and even seems willing to acknowledge the Puritan establishment in New England. As the century unfolded and ecclesiastics played less of a political role, denominationalism would become the classical low church-latitudinarian position, and dominate Anglo-American society. It was in reaction to this trend that the Tractarians sounded their first blasts in the mid-nineteenth century (see Church, 1970; O'Connell, 1969; Peck, 1933).

Besides the international, and sometimes eccumenical, correspondence of such figures as Colman and Kennett, the second matter of note in our consideration of Anglo-American interrelations is the difference in the position of the Puritan-based groups in each country. Bridenbaugh (1962: 62) observes, "In England the Nonconformists doggedly and unsuccessfully fought for their own rights; whereas their established New England brethren, already in full possession of them, feared the loss of a preferred position. Neither party fully comprehended the view of the other." Put contrariwise, the same is basically the case for the Anglicans, and in both, therefore, one should not be surprised to find different behavioral principles at work on each side of the Atlantic. In terms of the model, this would be the difference between tendencies toward the acceptance or rejection poles. In the American situation the Puritans accepted the world, admittedly, a world they created. In England they rejected it. The Anglicans, on the other hand, could never accept the rigorous New England establishment, while they were trying to recreate one of their own in England.

These differences of perspective are seen in the early difficulties of the Quakers who, beginning in 1703, appealed to the Three Denominations in England for support of the Friends in New England. The latter were being severely mistreated by the Puritan establishment there. The leaders of the Three Denominations were entirely sympathetic toward the Quakers and protested to the Americans that the very "liberty of conscience" for which "our forefathers" fought and endured the hardships of emigration not be now denied to these "dissenters" from the Congregational Way. Several years would pass, however, before the New Englanders would act favorably upon their fellowmen's plea (see Harkness, 1933; Sweet, 1965: 131-139, 144-150). In that struggle the newspapers would play a large role in introducing the church-state issue to a wider public than the ministers alone. The newspapers, according to Bridenbaugh (1962: 62-66), along with the pulpit would kindle many fires on both sides of the question. Through the press both Puritan and Anglican ministers in New England found that sermons might be preached in more than one place at one time. Ironically, when Kieth and Talbot first arrived they were welcomed by the New England Congregationalists because the two opposed the Quakers, with whom Kieth had been affiliated before he espoused Anglicanism. The missionaries' attitude towards the Quakers was based on an establishment Church of England assessment. Thus, for a moment the two establishments were seen to join hands against a common "enemy" to order. Only later did the provisions secured for the American Quakers by the English Dissenters become wedges for the High Church Anglicans to use in opposition to the proscriptions and disabilities the New England establishment had placed upon them.

To the Dissenters' credit, their homeland collaborators were quicker to appreciate the situation in New England than were the English bishops and influential peers. The misdirection of Parliamentary lay control of the English Church was clearly the most significant impediment to the advancement of the Anglican cause in the colonies (see Meza, 1973; Sykes, 1934). An understanding between the succeeding Hanoverian Parliaments and the missionaries to the northern colonies was never reached, and this held Anglicanism in a sectarian position there until after the War of Independence.

Apostasy and Episcopacy: The New England Scene

Yale College was the pride of colonial Connecticut. Its president was the most revered divine in southern New England (see Warch, 1973: 96-125). In 1722, that man was Timothy Cutler, a graduate of Harvard, doubly admired as an articulate spokesman for that "home grown" piety that was rising in New England Congregationalism. But, on September 12 of that year, Mr. Cutler astounded his brethren by concluding his commencement prayer with the words *"and let all the people say, amen."* Any eighteenth-century Congregationalist minister would find this phrase unsettling. It was clearly Episcopalian in style. And the next day, Cutler confirmed that his words were no mistake. He, Samuel Johnson, and Jared Eliot could no longer accept Presbyterian ordination and would leave for England to receive Holy Orders from bishops there. He claimed that he had "for many years been of this persuasion," even before he accepted the charge at Yale. The group would be known thereafter as the "Connecticut Apostates." "The aftermath of the great apostasy of Cutler, possibly the most dramatic event in the ecclesiastical history of the American colonies, was dismaying and shocking to the New England Congregationalists, who saw in this duplicity and treachery the approaching end of the Standing Order and the inevitability of bishops" (see Bridenbaugh, 1962: 68-69 ff.).[3]

With this signal proclamation, the religious situation of New England, and subsequently the Middle Colonies, embarked on a new course. Up to this point, the New England Anglicans loyal to episcopacy were an insignificant group, generally peaceable, and subject to the dominant mode of religious expression. When the Rector of Yale and his colleagues announced their "conversion," however, quite a different situation prevailed. The basis of congregational polity had been rejected by highly visible and esteemed "men of God." Cutler *et al* proclaimed themselves Anglicans not because of citizenship, nor for political advantage, but out of a conviction that the episcopate is essential to the practice of the Christian religion. They had embraced the *theological* principles of normative Anglicanism that the congregational establishment had rejected as merely diversionary for the past hundred years. They were saying "our forefathers" operated from false premises. The myth was a hoax. It is fair to speculate that if New England had not been under British rule, and if the "apostates" had not been so relatively numerous and important, they would have been exiled, like Roger Williams or Anne Hutchinson, or perhaps even executed. Instead, they received Anglican Orders, returned to Connecticut, and began a ministry there that was to be the major source of pro-episcopal agitation in the coming years.

The Apostates strengthened the other S.P.G. missionaries that had already come to the colonies. Together they worked to unseat any already established church and install themselves in an equally favorable position. Their immediate objective was tax relief. In the New England colonies, all citizens were taxed for the support of the Congregational pastor and maintenance of the parish church building. Until 1708, in fact, dissenters from the Congregational Way were not even permitted to worship as they pleased (see Bushman, 1970: 166).[4] People who came to listen to itinerant S.P.G. clergy in Connecticut faced imprisonment and/or a forfeiture of five pounds. The Reverend George Muirson, missionary at Rye, New York, who occasionally preached in Connecticut, summed up the situation in a 1707 letter to the Society:

> And though every Churchman in that Colony pays his rate for the building and repairing their meetinghouses, yet they are so maliciously set against us, that they deny us the use of them, though on week days. They tell our people that they will not suffer the house of God to be defiled with idolatrous worship and superstitious ceremonies. They are so bold that they spare not openly to speak reproachfully, and with great contempt, of our Church. They say the sign of the cross is the mark of the beast and the sign of the devil, and that those who receive it are given to the devil. And when our people complain to their magistrates of the persons who thus speak, they will not so much as sign a warrant to apprehend them, nor reprove them for their offence [in Seymour, 1933: 3].

Once the "Apostacie" had occurred, however, this feature of the Standing Order was seriously challenged. The Anglicans, Baptists, and Quakers together, by differing means, brought sufficient pressure to bear in England that colonial authorities were forced to relent. Beginning in 1727 (and finalized in 1729), these groups were freed from supporting Congregational parishes. Here, however, the Anglicans took a slightly different approach from their fellow "dissenters." While the Baptists and Quakers relied upon voluntary support, the Anglicans took advantage of a proviso of the statute and continued taxation, with the resulting revenues going into their own coffers (see Bushman, 1970: 167-168; McLoughlin, 1971). Apparently the Anglican ethos was not yet ready to accept the voluntaristic principle of denominationalism. Because of the differing historical circumstances of Baptist and Quaker versus Anglican persecution by the Congregationalists, the solution of the taxation problem would have different meanings and organizational consequences for each. The Baptists and Quakers adopted a protodenominational scheme (see Sweet, 1965: 120-166), while the Anglican Church in New England moved from the entrenched sect type to that of the established sect. It would remain there until the consecration of Samuel Seabury in 1784.[5]

Much more serious to the Congregationalists, and the Presbyterians in the Middle Colonies, was the now increased effort by the Anglicans on both sides of the Atlantic to secure one or more bishops for the American colonies. There is a vast amount of correspondence and publications relevant to this controversy.[6] A recounting of their details serves little purpose here. Rather we will examine the central issues of the debate. The major documents in which the argument drew to a head were Thomas Bradbury Chandler's 1767 *Appeal to the Public in behalf of the Church of England in America,* arguing the S.P.G. side of a non-political "primitive" episcopate, and Charles Chauncy's 1768 *An Appeal to the Public Answered, in behalf of the Non-episcopal Churches in America.* To the latter were added newspaper series by William Livingston ("The American Whig" in the *New-York Gazette*) and Francis Alison ("The Centinel" in the *Pennsylvania Journal*), which were subsequently circulated in England and published together with other materials in a bound volume in New York.

The anti-episcopal argument may be summarized in a few points. The first is that the Congregationalists and Presbyterians considered Anglicans in general, and the S.P.G. missionaries in particular, deceitful and underhanded. A second directly related point is the continuance of the anti-episcopal myth from Laudian days; i.e. that bishops are tyrants who will destroy Congregational "freedom." Third, no matter what outward pretensions are made to the contrary, a bishop in the Church of England hierarchy is *always* the servant of the State; therefore for the missionaries to protest that they wanted a "purely spiritual" primitive episcopate was, even if sincere, an impossibility to carry out. Fourth and finally, missionary zeal and English hegemony went hand-in-hand. As long as S.P.G. missionaries were Church of *England* clergy, they were obligated to the Crown theologically, economically, and politically.

An analysis of the anti-episcopal material, furthermore, reveals a great deal about the themes that were current in American life at the time and how these were woven into the anti-episcopal myth. First, the hated Stamp Act of 1765 stood clearly in the minds of the colonists (see Lucas, 1976; P. Davidson, 1973; Morgan, 1959). The tyranny that was imputed to the home government with the passing of this act virtually insured that the episcopate would never come about in its wake. Livingston at one point refers to "a bishop and his officers . . . a powerful spy." He is undoubtedly thinking of the Caroline use of bishops and their (lay) courts, out of the hands of popular control, to enforce monopolistic domination. He here suggests, with some "mythical" illogic, that the introduction of a bishop into the colonies would produce this same condition[7]. He urges that his readers simply turn to "a Church history or two" for confirmation of his arguments. References to Scripture, particularly the terror-inducing "compel them to come in," would delight the divine and warn the layman who had heard them often in sermons recounting the myth of the evil that lurked close at hand when prelates or papists

FIGURE 6
CHRONOLOGICAL CHART OF CRITICAL INCIDENTS IN
ANGLICAN RELIGIO-SOCIAL HISTORY

1675-1830

ENGLAND	NEW ENGLAND	VIRGINIA
1689—Toleration Act. Anglicanism denominational (from established sect).	1727—Repeal of tax laws. Anglicanism established sect (from entrenched sect).	1776—Repeal of tax laws. Anglicanism established sect (from church).
1711—Occasional Conformity Act. Established sect.	During Revolutionary War Anglicans as "Tories" in some areas forced into entrenched sect-like position.	1784—Petition for denominational status granted by Va. legislature.
1718—Repeal of Occasional Conformity. Denominational.	1785—Return of Seabury as bishop. Denominational.	1787—Confiscation of lands, etc. Entrenched sect.
		1814—Consecration of Bp. Moore. Established sect.
		1829—Election of "Asst. Bp.", Meade. Denominational.

began to exegete this verse. Though a Yale-educated attorney himself, Livingston capitalized on a combination of anti-nobility and anti-intellectualism to reenforce his arguments.[8] "The American Whig" said nothing that had not been brewing in colonial hearts and minds for fifty years or more, and perhaps that is why it was so popular (see Maier, 1974; Bailyn, 1967; Rossiter, 1956). The constant onslaught of these materials, however, gave a contemporaneity and an immediacy to old fears that militated more strongly than ever in favor of the pluralism of the American Way and against the possibility that an "apostolical monarch" from the Church of England should ever set foot upon American soil.

The crux of the argument between the Anglicans and the Presbyterians was over the nature of the Church of England episcopate. Charles Chauncy put this point most succinctly when he said in his *Answer* to Chandler's *Appeal* that, "It is not SIMPLY the exercise of any of their religious principles that would give the least uneasiness, nor yet the exercise of them under as many PURELY SPIRITUAL Bishops as they could wish to have; but their having Bishops under a STATE-ESTABLISHMENT" (in A.L. Cross, 1964: 182). The line was clearly drawn for the Congregationalists. As long as the Anglicans of North America were tied and under obligation to the Church of England, any bishops of that Church that they might receive were servants of the state of England, no matter what guarantees to the contrary might be provided beforehand.

With respect to the Church of England, the American Congregationalists were not by this time willing to accept even the broadest form of toleration. They wanted not the status of established sect, but that of a denomination. If that meant the adherents of the Church of England had to go without a bishop because they were unable to provide the necessary guarantees of their ability to function within the evolving pluralistic American social structure, then so be it. The Americans were, in short, demanding a total restructuring of *British* society before they would accept bishops of the Church. From the American point of view, as long as the Anglicans had any relationship of privilege with the government of England, their bishops were unwelcome. The matter eventually developed from here to the point that as long as English government had anything to do with American governance, bishops were not wanted. As Chandler himself had said in a less careful moment, "Episcopacy can never thrive in a Republican government, nor Republican principles in an Episcopal Church" (in A.L. Cross, 1964: 177).[9]

In all of the controversy, then, there was the continuing growth of the pluralistic denominational principle. Although it would take the New Englanders longer to recognize the full implications of their anti-episcopal fulminations, the arguments they were making against the Chandler proposal were essentially of the same mold as those to be offered by Thomas Jefferson, James Madison, and others only a few years hence as the final phase of the pluralistic coup began (see Sweet, 1965: 334-339; Beach, 1962; Mott, 1934).[10] John Adams, who figured centrally in the attainment of bishops for the post-War Episcopalians, in an 1815 letter to the Connecticut prelate Jedidiah Morse, assesses the pre-War setting and the change that had since taken place:

> . . . Who will believe that the apprehension of Episcopacy contributed fifty years ago as much as any other cause, to arouse the attention, not only of the inquiring mind, but of the common people, and urge them to close thinking on the constitutional authority of parliament over the col-

onies? This, nevertheless, was a fact as certain as any in the history of North America. The objection was not merely to the office of a bishop, though even that was dreaded, but to the authority of parliament, on which it must be founded . . . if parliament can erect dioceses and appoint bishops, they may introduce the whole hierarchy, establish tithes, forbid marriages and funerals, establish religions, forbid dissenters [in A.L. Cross, 1964: 269].

Thus the fear of Church of England "episcopizing" led to the articulation of democratic principles in politics and pluralism in religion, both of which entailed the downfall of the monopoly that the English Crown-in-Parliament continued to hold over the American colonies. A contemporary English writer foresaw the consequences of the current American attitude just as did some of the divines of Laud's day with regard to Puritanism. He wrote, ". . . some late alarming transactions, and the republican spirit which prevails in some of our Colonies, give too much reason to apprehend that what has happened in England [the Puritan Revolution] may happen in America, and that this rage against Episcopacy may be a prelude to downfall of monarchy" (in A.L. Cross, 1964: 213). Littell, furthermore, notes that Congregationalism itself could never maintain a monopoly such as that of the Church of England. "The New England standing order," he writes, "shattered on an inconsistency which ran back to its founding. A pilgrim church cannot be a successful establishment" (1962: 7). The lack of a strong legitimating structure for coercion within English puritanism as a social movement made it inherently incapable of providing any structure in America for maintaining a monopolistic society. In every sense, the "rage against Episcopacy" was a rage against monarchy.

The S.P.G. missionaries at the same time gave little assurance to the American establishment to lessen its apprehensions. Tied to the mother country for economic support, they also tended to mold their theology in forms more appropriate to His Majesty's England than to the First New Nation. Although a few made major contributions to the American cause during the Revolutionary War, the larger number either fled north to Canada, home to Britain, south to the West Indies, or into hiding. The bulk of the missionaries (who were *not,* however, the only Anglican clergy in the colonies) could not conceive of operating in a voluntaristic church organization, a denomination, or a pluralistic society. Throughout the period the missionaries refused to admit that the one thing that most of all separated them from the goodwill of the majority of their opposition was not their theology itself but the politics it entailed. Ironically, the more the Nonconformists preached against Episcopacy, the more the Anglicans "preached up" loyalty to the Crown. When the Stamp Act aroused the fury of the colonists, the Anglican clergy almost to a man took to their pulpits to oppose resistance. More than any other single cause, this drew the line for most colonists. The union and the threat of mitre and sceptre became clear. "The stamping and episcopizing of our colonies were understood to be only different branches of the same plan of power" (Bridenbaugh, 1962: 259).[11]

A Strange Monopoly: The South

We have already given some attention to the nature of the Anglican establishment in the South and particularly in Virginia.[12] Here we will see the continuation of the patterns indicated earlier and consider some of their further implications.

The great defect in the southern establishment was the absence of a bishop. As a result, and despite the authorization of certain clergy as "commissaries" to the Bishop of London for the several colonies, all of the functions normally pertaining to the episcopate passed into the hands of elected laymen. Similarly on the local level, many matters of parish administration that would normally have been settled by the bishop and/or the rector passed to elected vestries. In effect, the Anglicanism in Virginia was much more "Prayer Book" Congregationalism than the Church of England system. Although the Bishop of London remained the titular diocesan, his power to interfere in local situations in the colonies was practically nil. Indeed, even the picture of his commissary arguing with members of the House of Burgesses is quite antithetical to the picture of bishops that the New Englanders remembered from the Church of England at home. It is also small wonder that John Wesley and ultimately Methodism made major inroads here.

The one place where the Bishop of London had occasion to involve himself actively in the southern cause was with regard to the tobacco troubles and subsequent developments (the "Parson's Cause"). However, in these disputes he consistently sided with the Crown, "a fact which contributed not a little to hurt the popularity of the Church of England in the public estimation. It needed but a few such acts as this on the part of the bishop to convince even Episcopalians that their safety lay on the patriotic side" (A.L. Cross, 1964: 226).[13] The Virginians were learning that whatever the spiritual assets, a bishop could place more of a financial drain on a society than simply that of his upkeep.

There were some occasional efforts on the part of groups of southern clergy to secure the episcopate. These were in part due to the instigations of northern brethren, particularly the New York-New Jersey Convention out of which Chandler's *Appeal* was launched, who were chided by the Congregationalists' observation that in the southern colonies where the Church of England was established by law there was no desire for bishops.[14] None of these attempts got across the Atlantic, and none commanded the support of a majority of the clergy of any southern state. Indeed, it was impossible to hold a convention of a majority of the clergy in Virginia to debate the matter. The meeting that came closest to this was one of twelve clergy in 1771. After considerable deliberation this group voted eight to four to address the King *for* an American episcopate. In a month the matter came before the House of Burgesses, which passed a resolution "nemine contradicente" thanking the four priests who voted *against* the episcopate, ". . . for the wise and well-timed Opposition they have made to the pernicious Project of a few mistaken clergymen, for introducing an American Bishop: A Measure by which much Disturbance, great Anxiety, and Apprehension would certainly take place among his Majesty's faithful American subjects" (in A.L. Cross, 1964: 235; see also Bridenbaugh, 1962: 318-321; Brydon, 1952: 346-361).

To complicate matters further, the Reverend Thomas Gwatkin, one of the four minority voters, continued to wage war on the project. Similar to the Puritan clergy of the north, he asserted that it would be improper for a bishop of the Church of England not to have the power and prerogatives of an English bishop. In spite of being an "Anglican," Gwatkin did *not* want such an episcopal personage on the American scene. As far as the "episcopizing" party of northern Anglicans were concerned, Bridenbaugh rightly observes, "No Dissenter ever hit them harder than Gwatkin." He wrote to Chandler:

In the Name of Common Sense, who, or what, are the Reverend Gentlemen of New York and New Jersey, that, in this Protestant Country, this Land of Liberty, with such inquisitorial Solemnity presume to pass Sentence upon their Fellow Subjects! Numberless Passages in Your Pamphlet, the Petition, &c. show that your Intention is to apply not merely to the *Spiritual,* for the *Consecration,* but to the *Civil Powers,* for the *Establishment of an American Episcopate.* But this must meet with perpetual Opposition from the Dissenters . . . . In fact, there never was a Controversy carried on where Religion had so little Concern.

Bridenbaugh (1962: 320-323) thus concludes that, "It would be a mistake to assume, as has so often been done, that prior to 1774 colonial Dissenters and Anglicans shared no anti-Episcopal sentiment. Republicanism in religion existed in *all* of the colonies, not just New England. At no time after 1771 did religious differences [between North and South] stand in the way of political union . . . ."[15]

In terms of the model we see the gradual triumph of a pluralistic social system over a monopolistic one. "Pluralism means, then, not only the division into many different ecclesiastical organizations and theological points of view, but also a state of mind . . . defensive of it" (Mead, 1971: 257). What Bridenbaugh terms "republicanism in religion" is not far from pluralism, secularization, and the denominational society, nor from Mead's "religion of the republic" (1963) or Bellah's "civil religion" (1967, 1975).[16] These are the critical years for American religion (see Rossiter, 1956: 65-99; Morgan, 1956). The specific turning points are different in the various regions and have slightly different consequences for the development of the Episcopal Church in America. Nevertheless, what we see in "Anglican" Virginia, as much as anywhere else, is a rejection of monopolism in any guise. Although it would take some time for the pluralizing process to remove completely the legislation relating to religious establishment in each of the new states, the process was moving rapidly towards its completion. With the influences of the Great Awakening upon Congregationalism in the North and the rise of Methodism as perhaps the first true denomination in America in the South, the era of what Andrew Greeley terms "the denominational society" (1972), the product of secularizing Western pluralism, had dawned.[17]

Chapter 5
THE DENOMINATIONAL SOCIETY BEGUN

The Voluntaristic Principle

The period from 1776 into the first years of the nineteenth century represents on the one hand, a gathering up of the loose ends of the previous century, and on the other, the initiation of both new directions for religious history and a new type of social order in the First New Nation (see E. Smith, 1972; Marty, 1976). The dominant American religious attitude, pluralistic and secularistic, resulted from two ideological positions which, in spite of superficial opposition, combined to create an atmosphere highly conducive to religious freedom and the growth of denominational organizations. The first was the effect of the Great Awakening upon the development of personal piety, religious experience, and resistance to supra-individual corporate institutions. The other ideology was liberal-rationalism. Usually deistic and unconcerned with supernatural questions, this position saw religion as the great conserver of morals and ethics. Provided one were a "moral being" in society, one's particular theological persuasion, whether one even had such a persuasion at all, mattered little (see Miller, 1965).

Although these two viewpoints were often the major dividing lines for pulpiteers, both functioned together to bolster the concept of religion as a "personal matter," and of religious organizations as voluntary associations which one could either join and support or not. As the pluralistic tendencies that had been in this country almost from its first English settling were increasingly realized, voluntarism became the essential principle for religious organization. The religious groups most ready for this development were those that freely or by force already acknowledged the principle: Baptists, Methodists, Quakers, and New Light Congregationalists. Initially the Old Light New Englanders found it difficult to adjust to this changed situation, but its latent presence at the core of Puritanism forced it upon them perhaps in spite of themselves. Obviously the Anglicans, those of the church that had, if not its birth, its character-formation in the most strictly monopolistic of Reformation societies, had the most difficulty in coming to grips with the changed situation.[1]

As before, the Anglican situation in America divides into two camps, the New York-New England group and the Southern Anglicans. Each party would face different problems, and each would have to solve those problems peculiar to its own regional churchmanship before it could meet the other in a united national front. We will look at the New England situation first, then the South, and finally analyze some of the consequences of the American episcopate upon the Church of England itself.

"In Diametrical Opposition to Erastian Principles"

With these words Arthur Petrie, Bishop of the Scottish diocese of Moray, assured Robert Kilgour, Primus of the struggling Nonjuring Church, that Samuel Seabury was a viable and fit candidate for episcopal consecration at their hands (see Steiner, 1971: 196-224). How it came to be that a relatively uncontroversial priest should be elected by the clergy of Connecticut and consecrated by the bishops of Scotland as the first Anglican bishop in the First New Nation is, when stripped of its details, explained completely by this one phrase of commendation uttered by Bishop Petrie.

These chapters illustrating the model began with an exposition of the thoroughgoing Erastianism that erupted in England with the Henrican reformation. The union of the Church of England and the English monarchy resulted in the Bride being the seduced and submissive member of a pair totally dominated by the Prince. Subsequently the Puritan ideology, as the Congregational Way, became established in New England. The Puritans were "getting their own back," in Herklots' words (1966: 31), and the Church of England became an entrenched sect there far from the monopolistic privileges it enjoyed in Old England. At the same time, there was a shaking of the foundations of the English Church's hierarchy, with many of the most prominent Caroline divines refusing to take the loyalty oath to William and Mary. The same was true in Scotland, where Presbyterianism quickly triumphed, and the Nonjuring bishops became the heads of a persecuted sect of Episcopalians. With the "apostasy" of Yale's president and several tutors, the New England Church quickly entered a new phase as an established sect with certain privileges from the Assembly. Yet, the Connecticut churchmen were not ready to accept the New England Way. They used their small privileges as stepping stones for what they hoped would be an ever-increasing power base in American society.

The Revolutionary War crushed whatever illusions there had been in this direction. William White in Philadelphia put forward a "temporary" plan for the "consecration" of bishops by presbyters, after a convention in which clergy and laity voted as equals to select a candidate (see White, 1954; Temple, 1946: 24-28). The latitudinarian Southern Churchmen had never been proponents of the episcopate and so did not care, but the New England faction would not tolerate White's plan. For more than fifty years they had been proclaiming with vehemence an ecclesiology in which the Apostolic Succession at the hands of bishops in a historic line was essential. For the same years they lived off the fiction of the Bishop of London as their diocesan. This could no longer be, for by their own covert admissions, they recognized throughout their arguments for a "primitive episcopate" that government through the Church of England hierarchy meant more than that. While the Bishop of London might still be invested with authority from Parliament to ordain suitable candidates to the diaconate and priesthood, he could no longer be that diocesan spiritual vehicle upon which these Episcopalians had centered their faith. Yet the New England desire for an episcopate was not dampened, but warmed all the more.

An Apostolic bishop was necessary if the whole plausibility structure that had differentiated the New England Churchmen from the world around them was not to crumble. The worldly power was unimportant now. For the high church New Englanders, eternity hung in the balance. This is precisely the "exclusivism" element cropping up again, although with more accommodation of the larger system than in Scotland. Little's point about Puritanism noted earlier in regard to the Scots applies here too. It "... is not 'merely' the function of a social situation — a phenomenon that looks one way in one situation and quite the opposite in another. It is a coherent phenomenon that moves in determinate directions depending, in part, on the social situation." The model aids in the *specification* of these directions.

Undoubtedly, Samuel Seabury had little thought as he set out for England in 1783 that he was beginning the denominationalization of the Episcopal Church. Yet there can be little question that he was doing just that. A theological episcopate was Seabury's goal. He had no delusions of grandeur, and this may have been one of the reasons for his selection. As events were to develop, Seabury was confronted with Erastian bureaucracy at its worst. Certainly if he had ever had any real admiration for the Church of England ecclesiastical system, it was destroyed by his experiences there. With all the proper credentials from the people who were to be his ecclesiastical subjects, Seabury found the archbishops' hands tied by Parliament, and Parliament demanding (and probably knowing it would not get) Seabury to produce certificates of acceptance by the Connecticut Assembly. This body was cordial and perhaps even encouraging. But to apply to England for a bishop was too much to ask. "Let a Bishop come; by that act, he will stand upon the same ground that the rest of the clergy do, or the church at large" (in Steiner, 1971: 202). The Assembly had already placed all Christian congregations on the same legal footing as the Standing Order. On this principle the Episcopalians must base their activities. The clergy of the Connecticut Church agreed and communicated the whole matter to Seabury for the attention of the English primates. Again he was stalled. Even with the Archbishop of Centerbury's blessing, the Cabinet would not allow the bill (see Salomon, 1951).

Seabury's frustration brought him to friends he had made earlier who suggested he take up in earnest the matter of Scottish consecration (see Woodruff, 1940). After all, "Nowhere else in 1783 was there a body of Christians so closely resembling the Episcopal Church of Connecticut as in the region about Aberdeen, where the meager strength of Scotland's similarly named group was concentrated." By this time the Scottish Episcopalians were no longer being actively persecuted, and the Stuart cause had become hopeless. Membership totaled somewhat over ten thousand, probably less than half that in Connecticut. The clergy numbered about forty-five, "ministering to congregations housed in lofts and barns, in private dwellings and in plain, shed-like chapels." The Episcopal College, which governed the Church, numbered five bishops in 1783, the majority of whom "through a combination of Nonjuring and Jacobite logic, regarded the English Church as schismatical. Incredible as it may seem, these men considered two tiny congregations at Newcastle and London and the household of Thomas Bowdler of Bath ... as the true Church of England, these being the last remnants of that Nonjuring church whose bishops derived, in regular order, from Archbishop Sancroft and the other prelates ejected from their sees following the Revolution of 1688" (Steiner, 1971: 195-197).

The Nonjurors developed a virulent anti-Erastianism that turned them against any thought of *rapprochement* with their Church of England brethren. They managed this somewhat peculiar stance by elaborating the theory of Divine Right specifically around the Stuart cult, and then letting the two die together. The result was that the Church in Scotland to which Seabury appealed demanded above all that he renounce any Erastian principles he might hold, a renunciation that meant acceptance of the very pluralism to which he would return in Connecticut! In a final overnight conference between the bishop-elect and his consecrators, he must have done so, for the consecration took place and was followed by a "Concordate, or Bond of Union, between the Catholic remainder of the ancient Church of Scotland, and the now rising Church in the State of Connecticut," which in part reflected the Scots' feelings on this point (see Steiner, 1971: 217-218).

Seabury now returned home to his cure. On August 3, 1785, he was formally installed as the first bishop of Connecticut Anglicans. He thanked the clergy for their congratulations and for "assurances of supporting the Authority of your Bishop upon the true principles of the primitive Church, *before it was controlled and corrupted by secular connections & worldly policy*" (in Steiner, 1971: 224, italics mine). On October 29, Seabury's salary and those of all other S.P.G. missionaries who remained in America were terminated. While the state tax revenues continued producing some income through the early years of the nineteenth century ('til 1819), the Anglicans in Connecticut would generally have to rely upon voluntary support from the laity. This, then, marks the first confirmation of the denominational status of the Episcopal Church in Connecticut, and it is supported by all future developments there.[2] Much of the speed in accomplishing the transition from old nation to new nation for the Connecticut and New England Anglicans must be ascribed to the fact that the Episcopal Church in this area never had a chance to be church-like. If it were to survive, it had to move from a sect to a denomination, like Seabury's episcopate, "free, valid, and purely ecclesiastical".

Almost immediately after Seabury's consecration, he was asked by churchmen in most of the surrounding New England states to perform episcopal functions for them. He also ordained a limited number of men who came from the South. But this was soon to end, for there was a concomitant move, beginning officially with the "General Convention" of 1785 (New England absent), to apply for the consecration of three bishops for the American Church from the English line. This was an obvious slap at Seabury and the New England Churchmen. Since only three bishops were necessary for the regular and valid consecration of a bishop, the Convention in fact had to apply to England for only *two* bishops, with Seabury making the third. Factors of personality and politics on both sides of the Atlantic lay behind the decision to ask for three. On the other hand, Mills observes that it was undoubtedly Seabury's success in Scotland that practically compelled these other American Episcopalians to face the issue of episcopacy and take some action on it (1978: 242).

The prospective *episcopoi*, Provoost of New York, White of Philadelphia, and Griffith of Virginia, were each elected by their state conventions of clergy and lay delegates during the following year and likewise received the approbation of the 1786 General Convention. They also subsequently received official documents of approval (like those required by Seabury but which he could not get) from state officials and were benefited by the intercession of John Adams, ambassador at the Court of St. James (see Loveland, 1956: 159-160; Salomon, 1951). Due to the apathy and subsequent poverty of the Virginia Church, only White and Provoost were able to make the journey, and both were consecrated at a single service in 1787. By the Convention of 1789 a tentative peace had been reached between

Bishops Seabury and Provoost at the behest of White. Thus a fragile union was attained (see Mills, 1978: 242-287).[3]

The Consequences of Disestablishment in the South

The course of the Southern Church from 1776 into the early nineteenth century is amazing for the speed with which it practically decimated the Episcopalians and then built up again. The first step toward disestablishment came in the tax repeal laws of 1776 and following years. These laws moved Virginia Anglicans out of the church-like position they had held and into the established sect type. They no longer had a monopoly on the use of revenues for their own purposes from Dissenters as well as themselves. In 1777 the state-supplied salaries of the clergy were suspended for one year, but as a matter of fact, they were never again to be paid. Still the Anglican Church retained a quasi-official status. It was the only religious body recognized to perform marriages and entrusted with the duty of providing poor-relief through the parish system. Accordingly it also attempted to procure aid from the legislature. In a manner similar to that of the English Parliament of the early 1640's, the Virginia Assembly exercised its powers of control to weaken the church without severing the ties of their union (see Mott, 1934: 268).

It was not until 1784 that the Episcopalians' petition to incorporate as a denomination-like religious organization was granted by the legislature (see Brydon, 1940: 215-217). Yet the result of the granting of this petition and the subsequent "Statute of Virginia for Religious Freedom" of 1786[4] was not the end the petitioners had in view. A strange set of circumstances, perhaps best described as bucolic post-revolutionary revenge, catapulted the Anglicans toward a contra-indicated entrenched sect phase. Again in a way easily comparable to the immediate religious consequences of the Great Rebellion in England, a libertarian "monopoly" temporarily asserted itself against its own latent assumptions.[5] The historical manifestation of this temporary entrenchment centered around the church and glebe lands which by English charter were "owned" by the state. This was of little consequence during the pre-Revolutionary period,[6] but it was devastating to the Churchmen once independence was won. The Dissenters, primarily Baptists and Presbyterians, had long agonized that they had been forced to pay taxes so that the Anglicans could build "handsome" churches. This was doubly offensive because the revenue was also used to purchase items of ecclesiastical furniture that they considered *hindrances* to true religion. These lands and goods, they argued, now belonged to the state, not the Protestant Episcopal Church in the Commonwealth of Virginia. Eventually the Dissenters' opinion prevailed. The 1784 act of the Assembly incorporating the Church with its lands was repealed in 1787, and in 1802 glebes were sold to benefit the state (see Brydon, 1952: 492-507; Eckenrode, 1971: 130-155). The clergy were left without visible means of support, and their number rapidly declined. "Many churches fell into disrepair, and even sacred vessels shared the fate of the glebes, and often parishioners despaired as they saw a rapacious purchaser tearing down the old church to salvage its timbers. One marble baptismal font became a watering trough, and Holy Communion vessels were profaned [i.e. put into *secular* use]" (Albright, 1964: 151). The earlier persecution of Dissenters, done by the Assembly but in the name of the Church (much like Stuart England, again), was now being avenged. When and where it would end were still unanswerable questions at the start of the nineteenth century.

David Griffith never did succeed in raising the necessary financial support to make the journey to England for consecration,[7] and due to ill health eventually resigned the office of bishop-elect (see Brydon, 1940). The Reverend James Madison, president of William and Mary College, was subsequently elected, and a vigorous fund-raising project was begun, enabling him to go to England for episcopal orders.[8] The Standing Committee appealed to its diocese in terms that would become a part of the denominational-voluntaristic hallmark:

> It is not just, or consistent with the principles of our religion, that the generous alone should feel those burdens which belong to the whole of the society, and which, if properly distributed, may be borne with ease. We therefore earnestly recommend to all the friends of the Protestant Episcopal church, that they do cheerfully assist in raising the sum necessary for defraying the expenses attendant on the consecration of a bishop. Arguments the most pressing might be urged, were they deemed necessary, to induce a ready compliance with this recommendation. But we hope, that as you regard the interests of religion, and of that church in particular of which you are members; as you estimate the advantages which civil society must receive from a mode of worship conducted on principles most rational; as you venerate those instructions which so nearly concern your temporal and eternal happiness; and as you would, with a parental tenderness, cherish the best means of improving the morals of the rising generation, no one will on this occasion refrain from casting his mite into the common treasury. Let it, we exhort you, brethren, be no longer said, that we, of all Christian societies are alone inattentive to our religious concerns [in Hawks, 1836: 205].

This appeal was not overwhelmingly successful, but with some help from English benefactors, the voyage and subsequent consecration were effected.

Bishop Madison's episcopate was less than the boon it might have been to the struggling Episcopalians. Indeed, some of the most onerous of the anti-Episcopalian acts of the Assembly occurred *after* his consecration. From 1805 until his death in 1812, the annual conventions of the diocese ceased. Church buildings and furnishings had to be sold, and the adoption of an "itinerating ministry" from the example set by the Methodists (whose inspiration earlier, of course, was itself Anglican) saved the Virginia Church from probable extinction for at least a period of time. When the convention did meet, its choice for bishop eventually turned the office down, and it was not until 1814, with only seven clergy and seventeen laymen present, that a New Yorker, Richard Channing Moore, was elected (see Hawks, 1836: 245-246).[9]

Moore's consecration marks the passing of the Virginia Church out of its entrenched sect phase into the established sect type. While this designation admittedly benefits from the hindsight of later events, this placement is also justified by contemporary circumstances. The prostration of the Church by the "dissenting" interest in the Assembly had virtually run its course. That lands that could be sold had been sold, likewise the contents of buildings. The tremendous gains of the Methodists had taken their toll of Churchmen, but they had also made "bishop" a more acceptable title.[10] When Moore, a successful parish clergyman from a good-sized city with a history of stable churchmanship (see Klingberg, 1940; Morehouse, 1973; Greenleaf, 1846), accepted the election it signaled a definite change that would eventuate in a denominational structure.

There were hurdles still to be crossed. In the 1820's, for example, Chief Justice John Marshall was approached for a subscription for the Virginia Seminary, built during Moore's episcopate,[11] and replied that it was "almost unkind to induce young Virginians to enter the Episcopal ministry," for he deemed that the Church was "too far gone ever to be revived" (in Manross, 1938: 64). Moore and the clergy he attracted to him would have to surmount considerable difficulties. Yet he began with great optimism, and like the New England Congregationalists had done before him to prevent the coming of the episcopate, he would now find a basis in history, *myth,* for an appeal in Virginia to the "forefathers" and their faith to advance the cause of the Church:

> It is with the most sincere happiness I inform you, that the Protestant Episcopal Church in the diocess of Virginia presents to the view of her friends a prospect truly encouraging. The clouds of adversity which for years have overspread her horizon appear to be dispersing, and our Zion, animated by the beams of the Sun of righteousness, is recovering from her desolations, exhibiting the most heart-cheering evidences of returning health and vigour. In her restoration are associated the most affecting recollections. It is the *church of our fathers,* the sanctuary in which they worshipped the Sovereign of Universal Nature, and in which they expressed their grateful acknowledgments to the Redeemer of the world. At her holy altars we were offered up in our infancy to the God of our salvation. Hallowed be the courts which they have trodden and blessed be the altars at which they bowed in adoration! *Her children,* to their honour be it mentioned, *have not deserted the church of their fathers* in her distress. Though they have noticed with streaming eyes and bleeding hearts the desolation of our Zion; though the prospect of her restoration at one period appeared almost hopeless; still, warmed by the genial influences of filial affection, they have retained their allegiance to her interests, and preserved their attachment to her cause. May the blessings, the richest blessings of heaven be their portion; may the arms of Jehovah be their refuge, and his bosom their pillow [in Hawks, 1836: 109 *Journal* section, italics mine].

Like the Congregationalists, too, Moore interprets history in the way that most suits his needs. The fact that the "forefathers" were Episcopalian (in effect) in name is sufficient grounds for him to suggest that the present generation should be Episcopalians in deed. He conveniently fails to mention the numerous "un-Episcopalian" elements of colonial Virginia's established church. He also minimizes the lack of fidelity on the part of Virginia Churchmen immediately preceding his episcopate. His license in suggesting that eighteenth century Virginia Anglicans bowed at the altar "in adoration" is also amusing. This is clearly an anachronism of nineteenth century New York high churchmanship.

With time, Moore succeeded in instilling in the Virginians a sense of denominationalism, and a voluntaristic organization matured to take its place alongside the Methodists, Baptists, and Presbyterians who had already accepted this organizing principle. The definitive move into denominationalism by the Virginia Episcopalians is marked by the election of William Meade as "assistant bishop" of the diocese in 1829. While the canons of the national church had not yet created provision for a bishop coadjutor, the obvious intent of Meade's election was to provide episcopal leadership for the diocese during Moore's later years and upon his death. This move is significant in two ways. First, it indicates that the diocese had attained the ability to support a second bishop. Second, it shows the development of concern about organizational continuity, a denominational quality not at all present in the earlier years. Thus the "Protestant Episcopal Church in the diocess of Virginia" locally entered into the denominational pattern that had been set for American Anglicans as a whole by the General Convention of 1789.

Some English Consequences

One of the least explored avenues of religious history is that of rebounding effects — e.g., the influence of American church history upon subsequent European church history. The "critical years" of the Episcopal Church in the United States were not without consequence in Great Britain. Earlier in this treatment, we left the denominationalizing process in the English Church with the repeal of the Occasional Conformity legislation by the Whigs in 1718. The subsequent events in America precipitated further steps in this developmental sequence. The Church of England had to face the *internationalization* of Anglicanism, a concomitant evidence of the pluralizing process.

In spite of apologists who argued the English Church was nothing more than the "ancient Catholic Church" in England, a definite, though not entirely systematic, theological position, "normative Anglicanism" was being formulated. For almost a hundred years the "very insular" English tried to deny this fact by labeling the Scottish Episcopalians "schismatical" and establishing "licensed chapels" in Scotland almost as if they were legations of the English Parliament (see Steiner, 1971: 51). The American situation, however, did not afford the opportunity for such a maneuver as the still monopolistic Scottish Presbyterians did. In America the very idea of monopoly was being denied. There was no American religious establishment to enter into a diplomatic ecclesiastical exchange with other nations.

American congregations thriving at the close of the War of Independence were composed of clergy and laity whose contact with the Church of England as an administrative organization was minimal. As time passed and no episcopate came to be erected in the colonies, the American Churchmen, with the exception of those in the South, became more and more *theologically* Episcopalian. Forced by their minority position to justify their claims, the New Englanders particularly developed a very high theology of the episcopate,[12] one that placed "valid succession" above nationalistic considerations. As such, the majority of American Episcopalians were concerned more with the fact of the episcopate than with the locale of its succession. The recalcitrance of the English to consecrate Seabury led far beyond Aberdeen. When Seabury was received by his Connecticut disciples and subsequently by the General Convention of the Protestant Episcopal Church (see White, 1880: 29), the English were to learn that with or without their approbation *Anglicanism* was a reality. This denomination would "compete" with others not only in England but internationally as well.

As we have seen, it was *not* in response to Seabury's consecration that the English authorities consented to ordain White, Griffith, and Provoost. Rather, this service was rendered because the Americans met British demands. If anything, Seabury's consecration had a negative effect upon the American cause in England. Yet Seabury's consecration was not without its effects upon the English

FIGURE 7
THE PROCESSES OF RELIGIO-SOCIAL CHANGE IN VIRGINIA: I

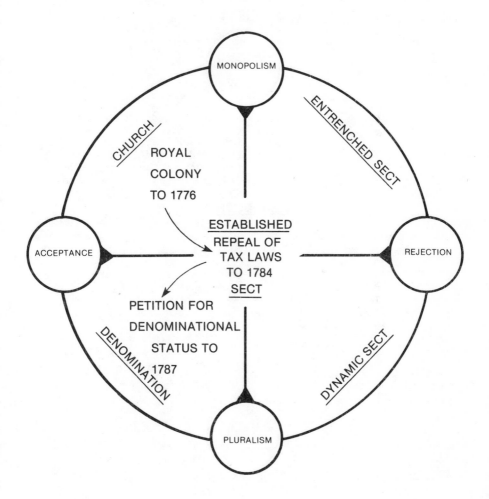

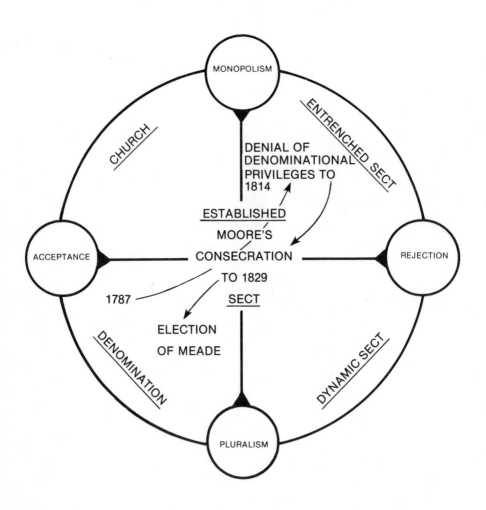

FIGURE 8
THE PROCESSES OF RELIGIO-SOCIAL CHANGE IN VIRGINIA: II

MONOPOLISM

CHURCH

ENTRENCHED SECT

DENIAL OF
DENOMINATIONAL
PRIVILEGES TO
1814

ESTABLISHED

MOORE'S

ACCEPTANCE

CONSECRATION

REJECTION

TO 1829

1787

SECT

ELECTION
OF MEADE

DENOMINATION

DYNAMIC SECT

PLURALISM

Church's relationship to the Scottish Episcopalians:

> This event triggered their Church's emergence from obscurity and isolation, for it created valuable contacts south of the Tweed. Scottish Episcopal theology subsequently excited the admiration, Scottish poverty and legal disabilities the indignation, of William Stevens, a leading London layman, and his cousin, Dean George Horne of Canterbury, after 1790 Bishop of Norwich. Equally sympathetic were Jonathan Boucher, Sir James Allan Park, the Reverend George Gaskin, and the noted theologian William Jones of Nayland, the last of whom enjoyed a Scottish correspondence well before 1784. These individuals, High Churchmen all, aided the northern episcopate with money and advice (at the same time extending help to Seabury in Connecticut). Their part in agitating the repeal of the penal laws — finally secured in 1792 — was particularly important [Steiner, 1971: 218-219].

This latter act served as the vehicle for the Scottish Church to move, in terms of the model, from the entrenched sect-like type to that of an established sect. An element of equal importance to the change in the Scottish Church's status was the death of Charles Edward Stuart in 1788 and the subsequent submission of the Episcopal Synod to George III as their sovereign (see Goldie, 1951: 70). It may well be, however, that Seabury's consecration caused a break from isolation sufficient to expose the vacuity of the Stuart cause to both sides. In any case, the continued tie of the religious and political systems and of external and internal changes in the relationships between the two is worthy of note. The denominationalizing process in Scotland was very slow in developing, but resumption of communion with the English undoubtedly altered significantly the position of the Scottish Episcopalians toward the Presbyterian establishment there.

A second consequence of the American Church's resolution of the problems surrounding its new status in a denominational society was that the English were confronted with this religio-social pattern as an acknowledged operational reality. The American Episcopalians were demonstrating that the Anglican system could be placed into "competition" with other creeds and not be dissimulated or destroyed thereby. Similarly, while it was not entirely consistent with the Anglican plausibility structure's concept of jurisdiction, Anglican, Roman, and Methodist bishops could co-exist on the same soil without civil war. In short, government could be separated from religious organization without society going to hell (see Walker, 1964). A realization of this basic secularistic principle lies at the base of any true pluralism. While the several Protestant religious organizations in England who professed their allegiance to the Crown had already achieved denominational status, England was hardly a denominational society. Roman Catholics, Unitarians, and various non-Christian bodies still were constrained from significant roles in the politico-social system. These disadvantages were removed in the nineteenth century, after the First New Nation had in a sense proved itself,[13] and all religious groups were given freedom to organize, while their individual members were permitted full roles in the political process.[14]

A further acknowledgment of denominationalized Anglicanism from this perspective was the decision, also in the nineteenth century, to begin missionary efforts in those areas, such as South America, where other Christian bodies had already "established" jurisdiction (i.e. were church-like). Generally this *missionary* effort, rather than a chaplaincy to Anglo-American residents, began in the United States and was subsequently accepted by the British Anglicans as well. Of course, the Church of England was already deeply involved in missionary efforts in its own colonies, but this hardly qualifies as an extension of the denominational principle. Efforts to provide episcopal leadership for dissenting bodies — i.e. "sectarians" — in Spain and Portugal, however, and a continuing relationship with these churches do give additional evidence of both internationalization and acceptance of pluralistic denominationalism.

A perhaps final consequence of the denominationalizing of Anglicanism was the acceptance of *voluntaristic* lay participation in the governing of the religious organization. Laymen as Parliamentarians had a significant role in the government of the Church of England as the Erastian principle was shifted from the Crown. A very important point is, indeed, missed if we do not recognize that at the very root of Erastianism is "lay involvement". Even the King was a layperson for that matter (see C. Hill, 1969: 41), although the anointing at his coronation was considered to convey sacramental graces that set him apart from his subjects in the eyes of the Church. The Scottish Episcopal Church with its government solely in the hands of the clergy was the only deviation from this rule. The difference between the American and English systems was not the decision-making power of laity itself but the relationship of the layperson to the organization. The point here has to do with the role the "religious non-professional" plays *re* the organization and the larger social system. In England the Parliamentarian served the state while making decisions about the Church.

In the American system the laity, in theory at least, served the Church voluntarily out of a dedication to the organization. Whether or not the laity are in fact motivated by "spiritual" impulses rather than economic or political ones, for example, is not particularly relevant here. The important thing about a voluntaristic system is that even if the motivation for the action were other than religious, the manifestation would be in conformity to the expectations of the religious organization and thus *appear* as dedication to the organization. The Constitution of the Protestant Episcopal Church formulated by William White gave the lay order in the Church power to determine the future of the religious organization independently of the state. White was chaplain to the Continental Congress and to the Federal Congress at Philadelphia. "Washington and Franklin were his parishioners; Hopkinson and Morris were his vestrymen; Jay and Hamilton and Madison were among his friends" (Tiffany, 1907: 299), and his role in giving shape to the denominational organization of American episcopalianism is attested by all histories of the Episcopal Church. Finding in his associates who framed the United States Constitution minds excited by the task, White devised an elaborate system of checks-and-balances in which the lay order was given veto power equal to that of the lower clergy or the bishops. At the same time, White guarded against the independent lay control that characterized the numerous Protestant denominations that were developing (see White, 1880: 402-406; Temple, 1946: 12-14, 21-29). While the latter move may have retarded the numerical growth of the Episcopal Church, it may also have served to reduce the tendency to schism and thus preserved its organizational integrity, with various parties forming order-like structures within the denomination itself (see Martin, 1966).

The American Episcopalians, then, introduced to Anglicanism the democratic-voluntaristic principle of lay involvement in church government outside of Erastian circles. The American situation introduced voluntary lay involvement to the decision-making process that was demanded for the effective survival of the denomination. Lay participation in the American Church was last to come in Connecticut and the other New England states. This may have been due to the Scottish example, or to the fact that having received the episcopate more rapidly than other regions, the idea of lay participation in governing councils there simply did not have opportunity to arise as it did in those areas where necessity demanded it. On the other hand, the partial maintenance of a tax-support structure into the early nineteenth century may provide an equally plausible socio-structural explanation (see Brydon, 1950). In any case, as an outcome of this a considerable change in attitude towards "the office and work of a Bishop in the Church of God" took place. Without exaggeration, it seems that the number of persons in the Anglican Communion today, whether bishop, priest, or layperson, who would list among the more important functions of a bishop "punishment" would be infinitesimal. The same is true even for "correction" as the seventeenth or eighteenth century Christian understood it. This can be marked as one of the belief system changes that occur as a social system, such as the Anglo-American, moves from monopolism to pluralism and the religious organization from churchlike to denominationalism. In a pluralistic society ideas of the nature, function, and even possibility of deviance and punishment themselves become questions for ecclesiastical debate.

ERRATUM

William H. Swatos, Jr.:

INTO DENOMINATIONALISM:

THE ANGLICAN METAMORPHOSIS

The reference to Richard Hooker
on p. 37, paragraph 2, should
read:

"... the eminent divine and
Anglican apologist *par excellence*
Richard Hooker could say ...."

Chapter 6
THE VALUE OF CHURCH-SECT THEORY

The Anglican Metamorphosis

The past four chapters have been illustrating a model proposed as a means of integrating church-sect theory into the more general theoretical context of a society's central value system. Specifically, I have tried to facilitate an understanding of how a basically monopolistic religious system developed to serve a monopolistic social system could maintain its plausibility structure at a high level of integrity, in spite of revolutionary social change, and thus continue to function as a pluralistic denominational structure in a secularized society. I have tried to underscore the interactions that were constantly occurring between the religious and political institutions in the changing sociocultural environments. In all of the detail that became a part of this analytical process, however, the primary goal has been to indicate how the model, in terms of both its content and its form, aids in understanding such processes. For purposes of summary convenience, this material has appeared in the form of diagrams at appropriate places throughout the book. We may now reconsider the picture that has developed.

In terms of the model, in England the Church emerged from the Henrican Reformation as a church-like religious organization. This development continued in spite of flaws in the patrimonial authority structure upon which it was based, so that in Elizabethan England the eminent divine and Archbishop Richard Hooker could say, "We hold, that . . . there is not any man of the Church of England but the same man is also a member of the commonwealth; nor any man a member of the commonwealth which is not also of the Church of England . . . ." King James VI and I, successor to Elizabeth, later uttered the prophetic statement, "No Bishop, No King," and with the major intervening variable of Puritanism, the bishops of King Charles I's court learned how intimate their relationship with the Crown would be: No King, No Bishops.

With the rise of the Puritans, then, from an intra-church party to an increasingly persecuted entrenched sect-like organization, and the concomitant heightening enforcement of monopolistic privilege in church and state alike by the Stuart establishment, the social structure reached a breaking point in the Cromwellian rebellion. The anomic situation caused by this thrust the Church of England into an established sect-like phase marked by the incarceration of William Laud in 1640 and ending with his execution and the abolition of episcopacy in 1644. This act, ratified and confirmed by the decollation of Charles I in 1649, resulted in the Church of England (termed "Prelacy" during this period) being forced into an entrenched sect-like status from which it did not emerge until the Restoration of the Stuart line in 1661. However, the Restoration Settlement as embodied in the Clarendon Code did not succeed in restoring the web of monopolistic privilege that characterized the pre-Revolutionary church-like structure. The Church of England returned to its established sect-like appearance at this point, confused about its corporate identity and its relationship to the larger society.

This anomic situation was resolved following the flight of James II, the installation of William and Mary upon the English throne, and the subsequent passage of the Toleration Act, when Anglicanism began to develop its denominational character in England. During the reign of Anne, this line of development was temporarily diverted by the introduction of the Occasional Conformity Act, which laid considerable disabilities upon Dissenters and caused the Church of England to return to established sect-like status. Occasional Conformity was repealed after seven years (1711-1718), and since that time the Church of England may be considered to have remained denominational in character.

In New England, Puritanism was established early in the Congregational Way. The Church of England (Anglicanism) as it existed apart from the Congregationalists was in an entrenched sect-like position from virtually its first days as a continuing religious organization in the society. It was not until the "Connecticut Apostasy" and the related tax law reforms of the early eighteenth century that Episcopalians moved into an established sect-like position. Except for a brief span during the War of Independence, when as sympathizers with the enemy the Anglicans returned to the entrenched sect type, they remained here until the consecration of Samuel Seabury to the episcopate by the Scottish Nonjurors and his return to America denouncing Erastianism and adopting a denominational posture adequate to the New England sociocultural system at that time.

The Anglicans in Virginia found their development much more similar to that of their mother-country forebears, although the Virginians never fully adopted the English system. The Church of England stood in a monopolistic relationship toward the other modes of religious expression in Virginia and had a relationship with the state through its Assembly-vestry mechanisms that made it clearly church-like in spite of the absence of a bishop. When Independence was declared, the status of the Anglicans with regard to their formal organizational relationships with the state became confused and contradictory. At this point, then, it moved into the established sect type. The Anglicans petitioned the Assembly for denominational status, and their petition was granted in 1784. However, hostility from some of their opponents in the previous church-like establishment days was not abated by this act. Unready for the full implications of a pluralistic society, these groups gained control of the Assembly in 1787, reversed the 1784 judgment, and catapulted the Anglicans into an entrenched sect-like position, where they remained until the consecration of Richard Moore as their second diocesan, when they again moved into the established sect type. Here they remained for some years trying to reorient themselves to the confused circumstances created by the deprivation encountered during their entrenched period. It was with the election of Assistant Bishop William Meade that the Virginia Church finally moved into a denominational type of structure and entered into national American denominationalism through the Protestant Episcopal Church.

My point throughout has been to urge that all of these analytical movements are not mere happenstance, but rather are directly related to the interactions of structure and content that may be subject to sociological generalization using the model. At the same time, I have eschewed simplistic cause-and-effect types of models that suggest that "thus-and-so" is always the causative variable and that "such-and-such" is always the result or product. Rather, I have suggested that there are dialectics inherent in all social reality, and that this quality must be applied to analyses of the relationship between the intrasocial religious structure and the larger sociocultural system. The dialectic that arises from this may be generalized into three moments which may be illustrated successively, but which are in effect simultaneously:

Figure 9

THE DIALECTIC OF RELIGIO-SOCIAL CHANGE

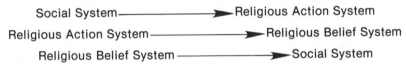

Social System ⟶ Religious Action System

Religious Action System ⟶ Religious Belief System

Religious Belief System ⟶ Social System

There is, of course, some rebounding to be expected in each of the moments. I have tried to show the dominant chord. This approach derives from, but is not identical to, that of Berger and Luckmann (1967). Omission of the first of these moments results is the error usually, though I think erroneously, attributed to the Weberian school. Omission of the third is that usually leveled against the Marxists.

The model, the data, and the dialectic all converge. If we look, for example, at the period from the ascent of the Tudors (Henry VII) to the death of Charles Stuart, what we see is a change in social circumstances as the Tudors win the throne in battle. Out of a desire to perpetuate this condition, Henry VIII makes certain changes in the church — e.g., the break with Rome, the English liturgy, the dissolution of the monasteries. This produces a belief system change, the tremendous elaboration of Divine Right, which itself, however, becomes the basis for the Puritan revolution. Although this is unquestionably oversimplified, it shows in clear outline form the basic processes at work. Similar illustrations can be found throughout the materials, the Half-Way Covenant being one of the most well-known American examples. In terms of the model, we may say that as long as the dialectic functions smoothly, religious groups will move toward the acceptance pole. Sectarianism is a movement out-of-phase with the dialectic. Ultimately it will be integrated into the dialectic either by changing itself or by changing the larger sociocultural system.

There are primarily two implications of this dialectic. The first is that there are specific generalizable outcomes of the processes of religio-social change. In short, church-sect typologizing is a live possibility. The second is that typologizing must take into account both sociocultural variables and religious content in order to be useful. This results in a model that is conceptually simple but that in terms of propositional theory-building requires considerable elaboration. My purpose here has been through the explicit delineation of such a model to enable the lengthy analysis of historical materials to be reduced to the barest essentials and so create an operation *Verstehen.* Here we can see commonalities and divergencies, structural similarities and differences, that occur in religious organization as it interacts in this dialectic with the larger sociocultural system. With a sufficient number of analyses such as this, we could eventually predict future developments in the religio-social relationships in any of a variety of settings. That, of course, is not at all the point here. Nevertheless, this model is a definite development forward from what past church-sect theorists have offered, and paves the way for future analyses along these lines. The best that the present work can offer is a different sociological understanding of historical phenomena and thus some additional directions in which to move.

One of the weaknesses of the current presentation is that it does not directly involve the dynamic sect type in the analysis. This is because of the particular organizations that have been dealt with and, at least in part, the time period under consideration. On the other hand, this type has had the most attention from church-sect theorists generally. Certainly it is not empirically vacant. Had we spent time on the Quakers or the Baptists in the pre-revolutionary South, for example, this type would have very likely come into play. Likewise, if one were studying the Mormons or Seventh Day Adventists, this type would play a major role in the analysis, while some of the others might be bereft of empirical content. Indeed recent break-away groups from the Episcopal Church, such as the Anglican Catholic Church, or infused with new life by Episcopalian dissidents, like the Holy Orthodox Church (American Jurisdiction), may provide for future applicability of this type even in an Anglican context. Had we looked at Anglicanism in an area that had not once been a British dependency this might have surfaced as well.

The model as it has been used here is not quantitative in its results, nor does it have to be. Sociological significance can be bolstered by quantitative data and tests of statistical significance, but it is not determined by either. Any such result must be amenable to interpretation and be integrated into a subjective meaning-context. On the other hand, it would not be impossible to establish quantitative measures that would permit such an analysis. Paul Eberts and Ronald Witton in an article dealing with de Tocqueville's morphogenic model (1970) suggest certain structural and organizational characteristics as potentially measurable variables of democracy, which could equally well be used as indicators of monopolism-pluralism. Techniques of content analysis made specific to the situation under consideration might easily provide indicators of the acceptance-rejection variable. Through a combination of these two measures a quantitative application ought to be achieved. This is not, however, a necessary step in order for the model to have value to the sociologist. Indeed, such quantitative analysis might lead to just the sort of reification that has imperiled earlier church-sect proposals.

From the viewpoint of "neatness," there is no question that the introduction of the established sect type and its use raise problems. On the other hand, a model should be as useful as possible in analyzing the empirical universe. In spite of its "grayness," this typological element is an important element in the model. If the Anglican situation is at all like any other religio-social situations, there are transitional periods in the development of both larger sociocultural systems and the religious organizations within them that evidence generalizable similarities. The established sect type recognizes in the formulation of the model itself that religious groups contain within themselves sufficient tensions so as to be able to move in different, but determinate, directions. Puritanism is *both* virtue and a reign of terror. Anglicanism is *both* comprehensive and exclusive. These antinomies validate a continuum approach to church-sect, and teach us that in the real world pure acceptance or pure rejection are as untenable as pure monopolism or pluralism. The established sect type captures, heightens, and idealizes this potential not as an "average," but as a case-in-itself.

Church-Sect and Secularization

At least as early as 1955, Harold Pfautz recognized the potential connection between church-sect theorizing and the concept of secularization. Will Herberg, who had already looked at one side of secularization in his *Protestant-Catholic-Jew* of the mid-fifties, attempted to extend Pfautz's work further in his H. Paul Douglas lectures in the early sixties. Here, too, he introduced a distinction between "conventional" religions — like Islam, Catholicism; the denominations, and so forth — and "operative" religion. A secularized culture is thus defined as one in which "conventional religion is no longer the operative religion in the sociological sense"; that is, it no longer provides society with an "ultimate context of meaning and value" (1962: 146). This distinction was to find continued expression in Bellah's discussion of civil religion and Luckmann's *Invisible Religion.* The early sixties also saw the publication of Parsons' seminal essay "Christianity and Modern Industrial Society" and the start of a series of works by Bryan Wilson, who continues to be the most consistent and prolific secularization theorist. It is of no little importance that Wilson has also worked in a way equally systematic and substantial on sectarianism — work that comes together particularly well, for example, in his *Religion in Secular Society.*

The same year that saw the "obituaries" for church-sect in the *JSSR* also saw two very important pieces with regard to secularization: Peter Berger's essay on the secularization of theology — ultimately followed and enlarged by *Sacred Canopy* — and a brilliant critique of pre-1967 developments in secularization studies by Larry Shiner. Like the obituaries, however, Shiner's piece seems only to have whetted the appetite of sociologists for more work on secularization. David Martin, who once suggested perhaps somewhat tongue-in-cheek that secularization be erased from the sociological dictionary, has now written a book that provides a positive cross-cultural model entitled *A General Theory of Secularization.* Daniel Bell chose secularization as the topic for his 1977 Hobhouse lectures. Roland Robertson's chapter on secularization in *The Sociological Interpretation of Religion* is one of the book's strongest, and some of these ideas receive further elaboration in his more recent *Meaning and Change.* Peter Glasner has written an engaging monograph entitled *The Sociology of Secularization,* and it is quite appropriate that the first volume of this series should be Richard Fenn's *Toward a Theory of Secularization.*

My purpose here is neither to present a systematic analysis of all of these different works or the dozens of unmentioned articles which they have spawned, nor is it to propose a new theory of secularization. Rather I wish simply to discuss in a few pages the relationship between what I have done in both my model and analysis and secularization theory generally. Here two things seem of greatest importance: First, the model is not a secularization model *per se*. Although not without similarities, monopolism and pluralism do not stand in an isomorphic relationship to sacred-secular. The second point is that in the West, in spite of specific historical variations from one sociocultural system to another, the processes of secularization and pluralism have operated hand-in-hand. Thus, within a Western context the model has secularization implications, but the general model is not restricted to the Western case and may be applied elsewhere just as profitably.

Church-sect can be applied to East European and Asian Marxist societies, for example, which are secularized but not pluralistic — as Mayrl (1976) has to some extent demonstrated — by dealing with the Marxist ideological organs as churches and by viewing all other agencies providing alternative systems of ultimate meaning and value as entrenched sects (in most cases, Poland being the most obvious exception). India before modernization can be seen as to some extent an example of pluralism without secularization. In spite of outward appearances, the recent turmoil in Iran may be viewed as based at least in part in an extremely high-pressured move toward secularization without concomitant social pluralism in a society where religion and politics were for centuries inseparable. Though it may be fraught with irony and paradox, the militant Islamic revolt was not without a quest for the freedom of a pluralistic society, or perhaps turned around, sacralization seemed better than secularization without pluralism. Many South American societies, on the other hand, are sufficiently secularized as to be able to permit religious pluralism but deny political variation — I think particularly of Brazil. Trouble occurs there for religious organizations only when, for example, Catholic activists get too immediately involved in land reform. Probably because of centuries of commitment to a Catholic sense of the nature and function of the church, South Americans find the idea of separation of church and state less capable of practical expression than North Americans of non-Latin origin.

Within the United States — as in many other countries — secularization has occured at varying rates in different regions, and at a sub-national level the model can incorporate these. Mormons in Utah and Baptists in the South have an almost church-like situation. Not surprisingly, these groups are more likely to speak out on political issues in these regions and exercise political-economic clout. In other regions, the mid-West and the Coasts, for example, they are more dynamic-sect like and focus their concern around adding members and a "private" moral code. Southern Baptists in rural towns often appear both for and against the world: *For* the world of their immediate locale, where they are church-like; *against* the ever-encroaching world of the larger social system. Catholics in rural areas where they have a clear majority influence operate in much the same way. Again, the point of the typology is not to label but to analyze. To call Baptists a "sect" or Catholics a "church" in some scheme that overarches the importance of interactions between organization and system is to miss the point entirely. Church-sect permits us to speak of relationships in an analytical schema, not to catalogue groups.

Recently there has been considerable debate about the limits of secularization. Herberg addressed this as early as the Douglas lectures, and both Bell and Berger have now taken up the theme. Again, my model does not directly address the question. Nevertheless some related observations may be made. First, it is clear from the analysis that there are limits to societal monopolism. Seventeenth-century England, eighteenth-century America, or twentieth-century Iran all suggest that "pure" monopolism is an intolerable social condition. Revolution is clearly predictable, although its consequences may be far different from those its fomenters envisioned. One might likewise hypothesize that pluralism, too, has its limits. The Glorious Revolution has been used from time to time as an example of a traditionalist revolution, and there can be no question that James II created a situation that seemed highly pluralistic. The debatable point, however, is whether the English really revolted against James' pluralism or the fear of a Roman Catholic monopoly as the final consequence of the pluralistic edicts. It is tempting also to think of Nazism as an anti-pluralistic movement; however the situation in Germany at that time was so complicated that such a generalization must be approached very cautiously. Ironically both Berger and Bell have been identified with the voguish label "neoconservative." On the other hand, it is difficult for anyone initiated into the sociology of religion not to think that some sort of civil religion, some unity within the pluralism, is necessary to the continuation of any sociocultural system. In light of this, it may be more appropriate and analytically substantive to talk about limits to pluralism than about limits to secularization.

If church-sect theory is to make the transition to maturity, it is to actual human interactions, social interrelationships, and institutional interdependencies that we must turn as the keys to our understanding of the wide variety of phenomena that have fallen under this umbrella. We may well find it necessary to divide the concerns that cluster here into several different theoretical models built around more specific interests. Questions relating to asceticism-mysticism, for example, or to why given religious groups emerge in the first place, come to mind here. I would urge that we keep church-sect alive for issues that center around the nature of the structural-functional organizational forms that generate and carry religious ideology in and through processes of both maintenance and change in the larger sociocultural system. If this is done in a comparative historical differential way, we have the potential for realizing the Weberian project anew. ". . . The knowledge of the *cultural significance* of *concrete historical events and patterns* is exclusively and solely the final end which . . . concept-construction and the criticism of constructs . . . seek to serve" (Weber 1949: 111).

NOTES

Notes for Chapter 1

1 Winch (1958: 11-116) persuasively argues that Weber was wrong in considering experimental methods the *sine qua non* of doing science. Nevertheless, this does seem to have been Weber's position.

2 Gustafson (1973) is of the opinion that Weber's typology was based on several criteria, whereas I credit this to Troeltsch. A careful reading of Weber (e.g. 1968: 56) will show that while he does at times elaborate the resultant characteristics of both the church-type and the sect-type of organization, the single variable remains the only basis for typing. Weber's elaboration is meant to indicate the kinds of concomitant empirical "marks" by which the usefulness of the single variable is demonstrated. Johnson's (1963) search for a single universal variable property is firmly in the Weberian tradition.

3 On Troeltsch, see Adams (1961), Reist (1967), Schwartz (1970), W. Garrett (1975), Gustafson (1975), Robertson (1975), and Steeman (1975).

4 Here I refer to the context of the sociology of religion. Roger O'Toole (1976), for example, has demonstrated the widespread use of "sect" in the literature of political sociology, particularly the contribution of Park (1967). Of particular importance to this discussion is his observation that Weber (1963: 135) himself used the term in a broader, not entirely religious, context. See also Eister (1973: 386-388), Gillin (1910), Mosca (1935), Martin (1966), Wallis (1975b), and Bryan Wilson (1967). The concept is also used (versus "school") in the sociology of science and certainly has applicability to the sociology of medicine and perhaps minority-majority relations generally.

5 Dynes (1955), Pfautz (1955), Moberg (1961), and Fallding (1974) are all examples of scholars who have in one way or another followed in the Niebuhr-Becker-Yinger tradition. Most empirical studies that have used church-sect as a part of a larger undertaking have also worked from this base.

6 Some examples of this are Peter Berger (1954), Coser (1954), O'Dea (1968), Redekop (1974), Welch (1977), and Bryan Wilson (1959, 1963, 1969).

7 See, for example, Beckford (1975), Benson & Dorsett (1971), Coleman (1968), Demerath (1967a, 1967b), Demerath & Hammond (1969), Dittes (1971), Eister (1949, 1967, 1973), Goode (1967a, 1967b), Gustafson (1967, 1973), R. Robertson (1975, 1977), Snook (1974).

8 There are, of course, a number of authors who have proposed more or less radical alternatives to church-sect theorizing. Because of my preliminary assumptions about the usefulness of church-sect, I do not think it important to review these here. Some of the most significant have been presented by Demerath and Hammond (1969: 163-195), Benson and Dorsett (1971), Gustafson (1973), Scalf et al. (1973), and Snook (1974). Only a year after the Benson and Dorsett article, however, Benson and Hassinger (1972) returned to revisions within mainstream church-sect typologizing.

9 Yinger also gets caught in this peculiar situation. In an early paper (1948: 314) he wrote that "the chief value of Troeltsch's work to the student of the sociology of religion . . . is that of a mine, not of a tool," and that "the sociological question . . . is not his central concern." Ironically, Yinger then excepts Troeltsch's "elaboration of the church-sect dichotomy" from this general assessment. His footnote to that exception is Niebuhr.

10 A transcendent referent is not necessary here, as long as there is an organizational form whose task is the maintenance of the system of ultimate meanings and values, i.e., ideology.

11 One of the best treatments of models is in Arensburg and Kimball (1972: 100-103); also see Ferré (1969).

12 The value of the concept "established sect" or something like it has been debated for a number of years. Johnson (1971), for example, is critical of Yinger's (1970) use of it. A careful reading of the former, however, will show that his major line of criticism stems from peculiarities in Yinger's specific definitional approach. A more positive assessment that integrates theory and research is provided both by O'Toole (1975) and Schwartz (1970).

13 It would certainly be much more *likely* to find church-type organizations in small isolated social systems. Particularly is this true if we work from Weber's thesis that the development of rational-legal bureaucracy is dependent upon the secularization phenomenon.

14 Geographic context is a relevant consideration. "Dynamism" may prove geographically mobile. Also, the model permits movement from dynamic sect to established sect (e.g.) *and back again* over time.

15 An article by Knudsen et al. (1978) illustrates the results of misunderstanding this distinction. Although the authors claim to be presenting a clarification of sectarian religion, their paper only adds to the confusion. It takes four empirical cases, assumes that they are sects on the basis of specious criteria, and then proceeds to test analytical models on the basis of these organizations! Furthermore since there is no comparison between these assumed sects and non-sects here, the results are practically meaningless.

Notes for Chapter 2

1 On Henry and Rome, see Pollard (1929: 367-375; 1966: 200-264), Hillerbrand (1964), and Byrne (1968).

2 Powicke has been criticized for oversimplifying a very complex matter; nevertheless, I know of none who thinks him wrong. Cantor (1967) indicates some of the complexities involved and their considerable roots in England's past. Certainly we would not want to push Powicke's introductory statement so far as to think that there were no other currents in England that contributed to the Reformation.

3 See also L.B. Smith (1953) and Simpson (1961: 1-21).

4 On Henry, Parliament, and economics, see Cantor (1967: 348-367), Dickens (1967), Elton (1972, 1973), Farr (1974), Kelly (1977), Lehmberg (1970: 56-161), MacDonald (1973), Parker (1966: 46-61).

5 The matter of "tradition" was one of the perennial controversies in Tudor and Stuart England, having ramifications in various social institutions. Little (1969: 167-217) in his chapter on Sir Edward Coke, the outstanding English jurist of the era, gives extensive treatment to the problem re law and economics. Likewise, Henry VIII appealed to "tradition" in his break with Rome, as did Richard Hooker when he denounced Puritanism (see C. Hill, 1965: 224-265; Tawney, 1960: 184-193; and Trevor-Roper, 1972: 244-245).

6 On the Marian exiles and subsequent developments in English Puritanism, see C.H. Garrett (1938: 1-59), Haller (1963: 48-81), Knappen (1970: 118-162), Olsen (1973: 177-197), Vander-Molen (1973), and Walzer (1966: 92-113).

7 On the parties in the Elizabethan period, see Collinson (1967), Cremeans (1949), Frere and Douglas (1954), Haller (1964), Leatherbarrow (1947), McGinn (1949), McGrath (1967), New (1964), Trinterud (1971), and Watts (1978).

8 As the Puritans became increasingly persecuted in successive reigns, the distinctions between the various parties became minimized but not obliterated. Seaver (1970: 8) observes: "Puritans of all varieties recognized a common bond of like-mindedness, but as an organized movement they present to the historian anything but the appearance of a monolithic party."

9 On the Settlement, see C. Cross (1969), Frere (1904), Harrison (1968), Haugaard (1968), R. Manning (1969), Moorman (1963), and Neale (1952).

10 During Elizabeth's reign (1570), Pius V issued a bull, *Regnans in excelsis,* after a mock trial of Elizabeth, deposing her and both freeing and ordering her subjects from allegiance and obedience to her laws. As such, all faithful Roman Catholics became traitors, and Elizabeth came to treat them more and more as such as the years wore on and her life was increasingly threatened. Note here, too, the seriousness with which the intimacy of church-state relations (i.e. having a monopoly) was taken by all sides (see Moorman, 1963: 205-207).

11 See Haller (1963: 224-250), Little (1969: 18-20, 133-135, 144-147), and Plummer (1904: 43-45).

12 See the important essay on localism, though written with specific reference to the Stuart period, by Breen (1975).

13 The importance of Richard Hooker, best known for his *Laws of Ecclesiastical Polity,* to the church-like position of the Church of England must be stressed. While he was manifestly the apologist *par excellence* of the Elizabethan Settlement and episcopacy against the Puritans, his work had much wider implications for the development of political and social thought in the ensuing centuries (see Marshall, 1948: v-ix; Orr, 1967: 147ff.; Shirley, 1949; and Voegelin, 1952: 133-152). Munz (1952) gives a comprehensive picture of Hooker's lasting impact, and particularly on the somewhat ironic relationship of Hooker to Locke.

14 See Ozment (1973) and Pulman (1971), as well.

15 On Whitgift and Puritanism, see Coolidge (1970: 21-37), Dawley (1954: 133-194), and Sykes (1956: 1-84).

16 Little (1969: 18) cites material from Weber in which he argues that the "ideal of patrimonial states is the 'national father'," a notion founded in "the authoritarian relationship between father and children." The concept of Elizabeth as a "national

mother" seems equally appropriate in this context. She preferred to think of herself as the "bride of England"; if so, she was a most domineering wife, albeit cleverly. Rowse (1950) gives a useful overall picture of Elizabethan society, although he does not handle the ecclesiastical controversies in sufficient depth.

17 See New (1964: 30-58) and VanderMolen (1973).

18 It is difficult to understand completely the English Puritans' optimism. Mary, James' mother, had been driven from Scotland by the "democratizing" Knoxians, and James himself had been imprisoned by them (see Goldie, 1951).

19 On James on the Puritans, see Ashton (1969), Goldie (1951: 4), Gooch (1954: 41, 59-60), Kenyon (1966), and Little (1969: 82).

20 "Law" used in this sense is not simply a written code or even common law to the Englishman; rather, it is a traditional "Way" to which is ascribed supernatural graces — almost the equivalent of the Hebrew *torah* — and that to which Whitgift refers when he speaks of the "wisdom of the realm" (see Little, 1969: 176-181, 188-189).

21 On the ecclesiastical economics of the time, see Bangs (1973: 5-16), Hart (1968: 19-28), C. Hill (1956: 39ff.), Stone (1961), and Tawney (1960: 137-150, 175-253).

22 This is, of course, an oversimplification. James did have a keen interest in theological debate, and this extended to his authorization of the King James Version. On the other hand, Charles at least entertained the thought of compromise with the Presbyterians in an attempt to save his life and throne. As an indicator of general trends, however, the observations in the text seem to be valid and in the proper direction. In particular, James' willingness to treat colonial affairs in terms of profit maximization rather than in terms of the extension of a sociocultural system provided the "loophole" through which Puritanism was able to get established on American soil.

23 Albright states that the establishment of the Church of England was a part of the *charter* of the Plymouth Company and cites an 1862 source. Stith (1865: Appendix I, 1-8), writing in 1747, quotes the original charter of 1606, and this does not support Albright's allegation. In any case, both versions support the fact that the monarchy intended that the civil and ecclesiastical monopoly be preserved and maintained in the colonies at their founding, even though no real efforts were made to enforce this until Laud's time (see Jessett, 1952: 302-305; Rodes, 1969; Tyng, 1960: 2-5).

24 The myth that the colonies that became the original states of the First New Nation were founded to provide religious freedom for all citizens — and did so — has now been well exploded and need not detain our attention further. There are several basic histories of the Episcopal Church in the United States which I have consulted and ought to be noted: Addison (1951), Albright (1964), Dawley (1961), DeCosta's introduction to White's (1880) *Memoirs,* as well as the bishop's work itself, Manross (1959), and Tiffany (1907).

25 The Court of High Commission may be traced to the Henrican reformation. It came into its own as "the" ecclesiastical high court during the reign of Elizabeth, and with its related machinery of ecclesiastical lower courts provided the judicial power behind James and Charles. By being entirely subject to the Crown's monopoly, the High Commission was endowed with the power to enforce the monarch's will at any time and place free from any legislative interference. The definitive work on the subject is Usher's *The Rise and Fall of the High Commission* (1913). Usually associated with the High Commission is the Star Chamber (see Cantor, 1967: 337-338; C. Hill, 1967: 298-353; and W. Jones, 1971).

26 In America the clergy generally were classed with the intellectuals. America has had an anti-intellectualism almost since its founding, but because the clergy and intellectuals were so closely tied, it never developed into the "intelligent anti-clericalism" that arose, for example, in France.

27 Detailed accounts of the Pilgrim saga are provided by Dillon (1975), Willison (1964), and Usher (1918). Stearns (1940) gives particular attention to the Dutch period, while Rowse (1959: 124-158) and Hall (1970: 53-72) speak to distinctions and relationships *re* Pilgrims and Puritans. The main thesis of Miller's work revolves around the relationship between the Separatists and (as he calls them) the Non-separating Congregationalists in New England. David D. Hall's introduction to the "Torchbook" edition of Miller is extremely helpful in clarifying the issues and suggesting where his analysis is deficient (Miller, 1970: vii-xxii). The bibliography that follows is quite comprehensive (also see Sweet, 1965: 73-89).

28 There is considerable debate over the extent to which this was true. Little (1969: 82-83) following Haller (1938: 3-48; 249-323) argues that questions of church reform were *not* the basic issues of Puritanism, but ancillary matters to something much deeper in the social order.

Notes for Chapter 3

1 The concept of "natural rights" is important at this point. Little (1969: 175-217) provides an insightful discussion of the problem from a legal standpoint, which is the apparent source of its popularity. Gooch (1954: 137) states bluntly: "The kernel of the theory of Natural Rights is ultra-individualism." The philosophical treatises of Thomas Hobbes are also of importance here, particularly *Behemoth* and *Leviathan,* which spring directly from the Puritan revolt against the Caroline monopoly. Just *how* Hobbes fits into the picture as far as cause and effect are concerned is a matter of some debate, which we avoid in great measure by looking at the question from a dialectical framework (see Warrender, 1957; MacPherson, 1962; Thomas, 1965; Burnyeat, 1966; Leites, 1978). Related to "natural rights," too, are questions of social justice and policy (see M. James, 1966; Kelly, 1977; Schenk, 1948). On the causes and effects of the revolt as a whole, the works of Stone (1972), Zagorin (1954), and the large corpuses by Christopher Hill and William Haller are all worthy of consideration.

2 See Little (1969: 81-131) and Richardson (1928: 260-281).

3 On the Independents see Curteis (1906: 39-80), Haller (1934; 1955: 189-215), Hudson (1955), Pearson (1969: 479-486). Tolmie (1977), Underdown (1971: 7-23, 45-75), Walzer (1966: 130-140), and Yule (1958; 1968).

4 This concept has a long and not altogether happy career in sociology that it is not particularly appropriate to trace at this point. I mean by it a more or less well-defined body of myth, doctrine, ritual, custom, and so forth serving the vested interests of a social movement, institution, or class (see Berger & Luckmann, 1966: 9-10, 19-46; Heberle, 1951: 25-32).

5 For more on Puritanism, see C. Hill (1965), Little (1969: 250-251), Miller (1961a: 92ff.), Spalding (1976), Trinterud (1951: 39-41), Watts (1978: particularly 15-16), and Westfall (1970).

6 The outspoken, persecuted, and often self-serving William Prynne may be taken as typical of the pitfalls that plagued the Presbyterians — of whom he was perhaps the

most vocal. Prynne rejoiced in the destruction of the episcopate and personally prosecuted Laud's execution with awesome relish. Yet, he opposed the subsequent political revolution and particularly the execution of Charles I. His more radical opponents answered his charges by printing a tract in support of their actions that was composed of extracts drawn from Prynne's *own earlier writings.* Bloodied but unbowed, Prynne determined that the Puritans had actually been infiltrated by the Jesuits (!) and joined many others in the Presbyterian party in hastening the Restoration (see Lamont, 1963; Abernathy, 1965). A more positive assessment of Charles' own negotiations with the Presbyterians when his defeat seemed near is that he was willing to compromise his principles not for the sake of his own life or power, but for the welfare of the country as over against a revolutionary government.

7 See also E. Foster (1970) and Mitchell (1957).

8 See Jordan (1942: 86-139). The matter of party divisions among the Puritans is a question of no little debate. Perry Miller in his pathbreaking *Orthodoxy in Massachusetts* weights the divisions very heavily; Morgan (1963) minimizes Miller's arguments as does David Hall in his introduction to the Torchbook edition of Miller's work (1970). Haller (1938: 18), in perhaps the most balanced statement, says: "The disagreements that rendered Puritans into presbyterians, independents, separatists and baptists were in the long run not so significant as the qualities of character, of mind and of imagination, which kept them all alike Puritan." A great deal of the debate, indeed, seems to center on the time frame of a given analysis. Long-run studies generally tend to minimize the differences between the groups and maximize the Puritan ethos that overarches them, while short-run studies do the opposite. I retain the nomenclature also to suggest certain sociological (class) distinctions that were very real (see Nuttall, 1957: 3-10, 104-107; Wakeman, 1887: 47; Yule, 1958: 1-20).

9 The matter of classifying "left-wing" Puritans is a difficult one. Some belonged to known groups — the Levellers being the most famous and influential. Others were "middle-of-the road" Englishmen who came to share a number of the religio-political opinions of the more radical groups. See Brailsford (1961), Capp (1972), Cohn (1957), Frank (1955), Haller and Davies (1944: 1-50), C. Hill (1971, 1972), Leites (1978), Liu (1973), Petegorsky (1940), D.B. Robertson (1951), Thomas (1972), Tolmie (1977), Toon (1970), Walzer (1966: 268-299), and Watts (1978: 76-220).

10 On Cromwell and the army, see Ashley (1958, 1969), Firth (1962: 335-338), C. Hill (1970), Howell (1977), Pearson (1969), J. Wilson (1969), Yule (1958).

11 Rice (1961: 72) presents an interesting practical application of this understanding of Christian liberty.

12 See Brydon (1947: 172-207), A.L. Cross (1964: 226-240), Herklots (1966: 32-34), and Sweet (1965: 29-33). "The Cavalier leaders in England, who largely consisted of those country gentlemen who were most attached to the soil, were less willing to emigrate than the Puritans. Thus, whereas the persecution of Puritanism (1620-40) sent many thousand Puritans to America, the persecution of Anglicanism and Royalism (1640-60) caused no corresponding exodus of Cavaliers . . . to Virginia" Trevelyan (1954: 433) states. Had it, Virginia churchmanship might, indeed, have been very different.

13 The debate follows the general lines I have already indicated. Miller (1970) was the first to raise serious question over the traditional explanation that the Puritans were "evangelized" into the Congregational pattern by the Plymouth men (see Willison, 1964: 290-293). Hall in his introduction suggests that the explanation may be much more complex than either theory and may in large part rest in the latency of Puritanism, thus making it all the more elusive (see Breward, 1972; Marsden, 1970).

14 On "liberty" in this context, see Bushman (1970: 3-21), Little (1969: 27-32, 128-129, 222-223), Miller (1956b: 1-47), and Morgan (1958). On the problem of adjusting Puritan liberty to American realities, see Carroll (1969), Miller (1970: 125-211), Nuttall (1957), and Ziff (1973).

15 See D. Hall (1968) and Polishook (1967), for more on New England dissent.

16 The Cambridge Platform constituted a norm, from which certain deviations were acceptable (see Breen, 1975: 21-22). The episcopate, however, was not an acceptable deviation.

17 On the Declaration of Breda, see Hardacre (1973).

18 Bosher's *The Making of the Restoration Settlement* (1951) is a critically important work in this area. Yet he betrays a confusion at several points in his evaluation of the historical data that illustrates particularly well the value of a model such as that proposed here. What he tries to say — correctly — is that the Church of England during and after the Protectorate was theologically stronger but politically weaker than previously. The established sect type handles the contradictions that make his assessments somewhat puzzling at times.

19 This was a logical extension of the political theory of Henry-Hooker-Laud. However, it failed to reflect their theology (see Lacey, 1969: 47-70; Schlatter, 1971).

20 On the Clarendon Code, see Hart (1968: 51), Hexter (1961: 71-116), Israel (1966: 593), Sykes (1956: 118-141), and Zagorin (1970).

21 In spite of attempts on his life by Jesuits and other Catholic sympathizers, Charles' continuous flirtation with Roman Catholicism made many Englishmen fearful of even the Anglican system. Christopher Hill (1966: 231) provides an amusing illustration of the tenor of the times: "The most memorable remark of Nell Gwyn, Charles II's actress mistress, was her rebuke to a hostile mob which had mistaken her coach for that of the Dutchess of Portsmouth, the French and Papist royal mistress. 'Be silent good people,' cried Nell, 'I am the *Protestant* whore!' The crowd roared its approval of her theological patriotism." Macaulay (1967: I 339-343) provides a fascinating account of Charles' death-bed "conversion".

22 James II was a professed Roman Catholic. As a result of this and for the greater exercise of his religion, he appeared, after some preliminary bloodletting, as a champion of toleration, suspending all penal laws against nonconformists, both Protestant and Papist. Charles II had attempted to do the same but was forced by Parliament to rescind his indulgence (see Boyer, 1968: 178ff.; Moorman, 1963: 262-263). Whether or not James was using his tolerationist tactics to restore England to Rome, the systematic consequences of his actions did not yield a favorable response. To the seventeenth century Englishman, this sort of "pluralism" was Papist monopolism slipping in the back door of the palace (see Macaulay, 1967: II; Trevelyan, 1954: 318-370).

23 Mary died in 1695. William reigned alone from then until 1702.

24 For example, when Matthew Wren, Bishop of Ely, was committed to the Tower with most of the other Laudian bishops in the mid 1604's, he insisted on remaining there throughout the Inter-

regnum in spite of many offers by Cromwell to go free. His reasoning was that by accepting the offer he was implicitly acknowledging the legitimacy of Cromwell's administration, something he steadfastly refused to do. At the Restoration, he became one of Charles' closest ecclesiastical advisers.

25 Partially because of his own anti-erastianism, B.L. Manning (1967: 111-113) is very sympathetic toward the Nonjurors. Christopher Hill (1966: 292) states that "many rank-and-file persons admired, if they would not imitate, the courage and consistency of the Non-jurors". Straka (1962: 29-31), however, disagrees.

Notes for Chapter 4

1 On the parties and Anne, see Guttridge (1966), C. Hill (1964: 87-93), W. James (1962: 103-108), and Robbins (1959).

2 See Brevold (1961) and Snapp (1973).

3 Also on the apostates, see Baldwin (1936: 5-7) and A.L. Cross (1964: 102-103).

4 I will generally use dates from Connecticut history in dealing with New England events. Similar dates prevail in the other northern colonies — Rhode Island, of course, excepted (see E. Davidson, 1936; Jessett, 1952; Midwinter, 1933; and Tyng, 1960).

5 I have simplified the time-sequence complexities somewhat here. To be more precise, the taxation move into established sect-likeness was followed with a move back to the entrenched sect type at the start of the War of Independence, then back again to the established sect type with the election of Seabury, and finally to the denominational type with his consecration and return to Connecticut.

6 For this material, see, Beardsley (1887), Bridenbaugh (1962: 74-281), Cameron (1970; 1972), Carroll (1970), A.L. Cross (1964: 107-348), Ellis (1973), Ferm (1969: 98-107), Gaustad (1968: 49-63), W. Nelson (1909), Schneider and Schneider (1929), P. Smith (1976), and J. Wilson (1965).

7 The Stamp Act was connected to the episcopate in the minds of many Americans because it required that offenders against its provisions be tried in *admiralty courts,* i.e., by officers of the Crown-in-Parliament without juries. The colonists saw this move to circumvent local justice as likely to be extended to ecclesiastical courts, if ever bishops were to be sent. In addition, when the Stamp Act was repealed, Parliament passed the Declaratory Act of 1766, which asserted its sovereign power "to make Laws . . . to bind the Colonists and People of America . . . in all Cases whatsoever." Because this act was passed under the Pitt ministry, toward which the Americans were generally favorable, it was initially regarded by most as merely a face-saving device and not a cause for concern. Continued developments, however, demonstrated that this preliminary assessment was euphoric, and the power of King and Parliament in the colonies hence became a matter for ever-increasing apprehension (see Maier, 1974; Morgan, 1959).

8 Eduard Bernstein (1963: 236) notes that the communistic sects of seventeenth-century England showed in like manner "a contempt for academic learning combined with a great interest in education."

9 Even though the Church of England was relatively denominationalized at home, the social system it was "accepting" was quite different from that which had developed in America. Just as there may be a wide variety of sectarian experiences (see Wallis, 1975b: 9-14), so denominationalism must not be restricted to one particular socio-historical context or expression. This is an essential point in understanding what is involved in a comparative ideal-typical analysis.

10 The apparent development was from the Independents to James Harrington to John Locke to Jefferson, with a good smattering of lawyers as catalytic agents. Even Wills (1978), who minimizes Locke's influence on Jefferson's ideas generally, acknowledges it with regard to religion. Also see Cranston (1969), Dunn (1969), and Gooch (1954).

11 See Baldwin (1936: 6-12), A.L. Cross (1964: 159), and Morgan (1959).

12 Virginia forms a paradigm for the southern colonies here, as Connecticut does for New England. See Clarke (1976), Dalcho (1972), E. Davidson (1936), Rodgers (1959), and Strickland (1939).

13 For more on the Parson's Cause, see Eckenrode (1971: 20-30), Foote (1966: 310ff.), Hawks (1936: 114-131), and Sweet (1965: 29-33).

14 The Congregationalists also like to point out that, whereas they had freed the Anglicans and others from their establishment tax burdens at the beginning of the eighteenth century, the southern Anglicans had not accorded Presbyterians or other dissenters there the same privilege (see Bridenbaugh, 1962: 11; Pilcher, 1971).

15 See Maier (1974) for more on pre-revolutionary solidarity.

16 See Albanese (1976) for civil religion and the revolution.

17 I will not deal with the various phenomena of the Great Awakening and its aftermath in any direct way, since a treatment of these is not particularly necessary to the development of the basic argument or to the illustration of the model. Nevertheless, the importance of the Awakening to the overall course of events in American religious history is not to be minimized. Indeed, it is essential that we recognize that the Awakening had political and social consequences that extended far beyond outpourings of personal piety. As Bushman (1970: 220) argues, "The truly revolutionary aspect of the Awakening was the dilution of divine sanction in traditional institutions and the investiture of authority in some inward experience. Thereby the church lost power, and individuals gained it, using it to reform the old order in both principle and practice. The final outcome, though largely unintentional, was to enlarge religious liberty." The piety of the Awakening thus contributed significantly to the politics of American pluralism (see further, Bushman, 1970: 183-220; Gaustad, 1957; Heimert and Miller, 1967; Miller, 1961b; Sweet, 1965: 311-318). Niebuhr and Heimert (1963: 17) note the "revolutionary" significance of the Great Awakening, too, "as an instrument and symbol of intercolonial solidarity of Presbyterians, Baptists, and 'New Lights' from New Hampshire to Georgia." There has lately been a renewed interest in the work and person of Jonathan Edwards, with reprints of almost all his writings becoming available. The Wesleys and George Whitefield are also important figures. With the exception of a few studies on Methodism, however, little of this work gives attention to the latent functions of the Awakening noted here.

Notes for Chapter 5

1 The conclusions of J.J. Mol's study of the adjustment tensions of Dutch and German clergy in early eighteenth century America (1968) complement mine: Clergy from "free" bodies adjusted better than those from national establishments. His study would be amenable to the model proposed here and show patterns similar to this one.

2 I disagree with Bushman (1970: 223) when he says, "After 1765 the Anglicans and Baptists and to a lesser degree the Separates were not simply dissenters but denominations." Although he never specifies precisely the meaning of his concept "denomination," he fails completely to

account for the voluntaristic principle and its retarded growth among Anglicans.

3 An interesting sidelight of Anglo-American exchange is that the first wife of John Moore, the Archbishop of Canterbury who consecrated White and Provoost, was the daughter of a chief justice of South Carolina. One would suspect that Moore's reluctance to consecrate for the Americans without evidences that they would be well-received by the general populace may have been based on first hand testimony of Southern opposition to the episcopate.

4 This act is quoted in full by Hawks (1836: 175-177), who gives its actual date of passage as December 26, 1785. The statute was largely, if not entirely, the work of Thomas Jefferson and one of his works that pleased him most — though he was in France when it was passed (see Sperry, 1946: 44-45). Said to be "the first law ever passed by a popular Assembly giving perfect freedom of conscience," this act is perhaps the statement *sine qua non* of the logic underlying the secularistic denominational principle of voluntarism. For background, see Gaustad (1969), Hood (1971), Lindsay (1962: 121-123), Little (1974b, 1976), Marty (1976), Rainbolt (1975), E. Smith (1972). On the role of James Madison, see Mott (1934: particularly 268).

5 The disestablishment of the New England churches was not fraught with "backlash" tendencies. Can we say that, comparing the Caroline and Virginian situations on the one hand with the New England Puritan on the other, the degree of latent monopolism or pluralism in a religious system will be a determinant of the amount of social upheaval involved in changing from one type of central value system to another in the larger society?

6 I use the phrase "little consequence" in a relative way. *If* the home government had, for example, seen fit to invest control in the hands of the clergy, the implications might have been quite significant, not only for the present controversy but also for the political situation in general.

7 Mills (1978: 243) notes the strong opposition to a bishop that persisted among Virginia Episcopalians even after the war. Griffith was elected by the absolute minimum number of votes possible at the convention. Indeed, White wrote in 1782 that "there cannot be produced an instance of laymen . . . soliciting the introduction of a bishop; it was probably by a great majority of them thought an hazardous experiment" (in Mills, 1978: 185-186).

8 Exactly why Madison and his Virginia constituency valued English consecration so highly (with three bishops already in America) is not entirely clear. Apparently the English had insisted originally that because of the political elements surrounding the Scots, Seabury's orders were questionable and agreed to consecrate for the Americans only if three bishops were ordained at their hands. Many American Episcopalians felt the same way. Subsequently, however, the Americans had agreed that Seabury's orders were beyond dispute, and White and Provoost held English orders already. Thus White, Provoost, and Seabury could have consecrated Madison without nearly the expense or hazard of a trip to England. The probable resolution of the problem is that the Americans felt bound to honor the agreement with the English on its original terms.

9 To give these figures a little more meaning: The Convention *Journal* (see Hawks, 1836) of the 1785 session shows 36 clergy and 71 laymen attending. In 1786 they decline to 16 and 47 respectively. In 1790, 27 and 33. By 1805, 15 and 16; 1812, 13 and 12; 1813, 8 and 9. Albright (1964: 150) estimates that in 1775 there were about 95 clergy and parishes with a total of 164 churches and chapels. Similarly, in South Carolina (see Clarke, 1976: 25-27), Robert Smith was elected and consecrated the first bishop in 1795. After his death in 1801, more than ten years would pass before the election of the second bishop. Also, in the early days of the Episcopal Church, a bishop did not cease to hold parochial duties in a local congregation. This type of arrangement was precisely that which the right-wing Puritans of the sixteenth and seventeenth centuries, those still willing to hold to some form of episcopate, attempted to create in the Church of England at that time.

10 Both A.L. Cross (1964: 267) and Mott (1934: 268) suggest that if the Virginia Anglicans had not had the demands of an establishment placed upon them, a union might have been maintained between themselves and the Methodists. Because of the tremendous impact of Methodism upon subsequent religious developments in America — and England, for that matter — this is a point of some importance. If the Methodist schism could have been avoided, or the breach rapidly repaired, the religio-social scene in Anglo-American society today might be very different. White also attempted to create a workable arrangement with Wesley, but was not successful (see Mills, 1978: 252-256).

11 Before he was a bishop but while he was president of William and Mary, Madison had agreed with the decision to delete the divinity school from that institution (see Mills, 1978: 284).

12 Mills (1978) argues that the Americans chose a "low-church form of episcopacy," with bishops elected by their flocks and separated from the state. He is both right and wrong. In the colonies where the Church was strongest, the Americans had a relatively high doctrine of the episcopate *qua* episcopate, but their society's central value system was pluralistic and denominational, thus the synthesis of Laudian ("high

church") and latitudinarian ("low church") perspectives. It is of more than passing antiquarian interest that the only Anglican bishops known to use mitres in the period from 1785 to the Oxford revival, and their use was *very* rare throughout the eighteenth century, were Americans: Seabury and Claggett of Maryland (see Cameron, 1970; Thoms, 1963). Elected bishops who wore mitres were much more ancient, Catholic, and theologically "high church" than Erastian administrators.

13 The many travelers' reports that came back to Europe from visitors to America, for example (see Lipset, 1967: 159-192), are evidences of the more than passing interest of Europeans in the American experiment, particularly in matters of religion. America was in many ways a testing ground for life styles later adopted in, though adapted to, Europe.

14 Though his analysis is generally quite sound, Bryan Wilson (1966) somewhat overstates the case for the comparability of British and American secularization processes. The continued teaching of religion in the schools, the intimacy of the Archbishop's presence to the royal-political process, and the technical establishment of one denomination all make Great Britain less secularized (also see Martin, 1967). Garrison (1948: 15) notes, "A Jew received an honorary degree from Harvard in 1720 — and that was 150 years before Oxford would admit a Jew to a degree" (also see Soloway, 1969; K. Thompson, 1970: 1-11). We ought to note, too, the importance of Methodism for the English social system (see J. Foster, 1974; Halévy, 1971: 33-77; E.P. Thompson, 1963). On the other hand, Methodism is only properly understood as an Anglo-*American* phenomenon.

BIBLIOGRAPHY

Throughout the text citations, references are to the edition actually consulted. When that volume is a reprint of a much earlier work, the original date is indicated here in brackets, following the citation.

The following conventions have been adopted:

1). Several journal titles are abbreviated:

ASR   *American Sociological Review*
CH   *Church History*
HM   *Historical Magazine of the Protestant Episcopal Church*
JSSR   *Journal for the Scientific Study of Religion*
JCS   *Journal of Church and State*
SA   *Sociological Analysis*

2). Except where the entry would become senseless, the words "press," "publishers," "publications," and so forth have been dropped from the publication data. In most cases, university presses are simply entered by the name of the school with which they are associated — i.e., "Chicago" for the University of Chicago, "Cambridge" for Cambridge University, "Tennessee" for the University of Tennessee.

3). Subtitles, translators' names, and so forth are generally omitted. If more than one article from an edited collection is included, the volume receives a separate entry and is cited with a given article merely by author/editor and year of publication.

Abernathy, G.R., Jr.
1965 *The English Presbyterians and the Stuart Restoration.* Philadelphia: American Philosophical Society.

Abramowski, Günter
1966 *Das Geschichtsbild Max Webers.* Stuttgart: Klett.

Adams, James Luther
1961 "Ernst Troeltsch as Analyst of Religion." *JSSR* 1: 98-109.
1971 "The Voluntary Principle in the Forming of American Religion." Pp. 217-246 in E.A. Smith, 1971.

Addison, James Thayer
1951 *The Episcopal Church in the United States.* New York: Scribners.
1952 "William Laud, Prelate and Champion of Order." *HM* 21: 17-61.

Ahlstrom, Sydney E.
1970 "The Problem of the History of Religion in America." *CH* 39: 224-235.
1972 *A Religious History of the American People.* New Haven: Yale.

Aiken, William A. and Basil D. Henning
1970 (eds.).*Conflict in Stuart England.* Hamden, Ct.: Archon [1960].

Albanese, Catherine L.
1976 *Sons of the Fathers.* Philadelphia: Temple.

Albright, Raymond W.
1964 *A History of the Protestant Episcopal Church.* New York: Macmillan.

Alford, Robert R.
1963 *Party and Society.* Chicago: Rand-McNally.

Anson, Peter F.
1964 *Bishops at Large.* London: Faber and Faber.

Arensburg, Conrad M. and Solon T. Kimball.
1972 *Culture and Community.* Gloucester, Mass.: Smith.

Ashley, Maurice.
1958 *Oliver Cromwell and the Puritan Revolution.* London: English Universities.
1969 (ed.). *Cromwell.* Englewood Cliffs, N.J.: Prentice-Hall.

Ashton, Robert.
1969 (ed.). *James I by his Contemporaries.* London: Hutchinson.

Aylmer, G.E.
1972 (ed.). *The Interregnum.* Hamden, Ct.: Archon.

Bailyn, Bernard.
1967 *The Ideological Origins of the American Revolution.* Cambridge: Harvard.

Baldwin, Alice Mary.
1928 *The New England Clergy and the American Revolution.* Durham, N.C.: Duke.
1936 *The Clergy of Connecticut in Revolutionary Days.* New Haven: Yale.

Bangs, Carl.
1973 " 'All the Best Bishoprics and Deaneries': The Enigma of Arminian Politics." *CH* 42: 5-16.

Beach, Waldo.
1962 "Sectarianism and Skepticism." Pp. 199-211 in Franklin H. Littell (ed.), *Reformation Studies.* Richmond: John Knox.

Beardsley, E. Edwards.
1887 *Life and Correspondence of Samuel Johnson, D.D.*, 3rd. ed. Boston: Houghton-Mifflin.

Becker, Howard.
1932 *Systematic Sociology.* New York: Wiley.

Beckford, James A.
1975 *The Trumpet of Prophecy.* New York: Wiley.

Bell, Daniel.
1977 "The Return of the Sacred? The Argument on the Future of Religion." *British Journal of Sociology* 28: 419-449.

Bellah, Robert N.
1967 "Civil Religion in America." *Daedalus* 96: 1-19.
1975 *The Broken Covenant.* New York: Seabury.

Bennett, G.V.
1966 "King William III and the Episcopate." Pp. 104-131 in Bennett and Walsh, 1966.
1969 "Conflict in the Church." Pp. 155-175 in Geoffrey Holmes (ed.), *Britain after the Glorious Revolution*. London: Macmillan.

Bennett, G.V. and J.D. Walsh.
1966 (eds.). *Essays in Modern Church History*. New York: Oxford.

Benson, J. Kenneth and James H. Dorsett.
1971 "Toward a Theory of Religious Organizations." *JSSR* 10: 138-151.

Benson, J. Kenneth and Edward W. Hassinger.
1972 "Organization Set and Resources as Determinants of Formalization in Religious Organizations." *Review of Religious Research* 14: 30-36.

Berger, Peter L.
1954 "The Sociological Study of Sectarianism." *Social Research* 21: 467-485.
1969 *The Sacred Canopy*. Garden City, N.Y.: Doubleday/Anchor.
1970 *A Rumor of Angels*. Garden City, N.Y.: Doubleday/Anchor.
1977 "'A Great Revival' Coming for America's Churches." *U.S. News & World Report* 82 (April 11): 70-72.

Berger, Peter L. and Thomas Luckmann
1967 *The Social Construction of Reality*. Garden City, N.Y.: Doubleday/Anchor.

Berger, Stephen D.
1971 "The Sects and the Breakthrough into the Modern World." *Sociological Quarterly* 12: 486-499.

Bernstein, Eduard.
1963 *Cromwell and Communism*. New York: Schocken [1895].

Best, G.F.A.
1964 *Temporal Pillars*. Cambridge.

Bosher, Robert S.
1951 *The Making of the Restoration Settlement*. New York: Oxford.

Bottomore, T.B.
1971 *Sociology*. New York: Random House.

Boyer, Paul and Stephen Nissenbaum.
1974 *Salem Possessed*. Cambridge: Harvard.

Boyer, Richard E.
1968 *English Declarations of Indulgence, 1687 and 1688*. The Hague: Moulton.

Brailsford, H.N.
1961 *The Levellers and the English Revolution* (ed. C. Hill). Palo Alto, Ca.: Stanford.

Breen, T.H.
1975 "Persistent Localism." *William and Mary Quarterly* 32: 3-28.

Brevold, Louis I.
1961 *The Brave New World of the Enlightenment*. Ann Arbor: Michigan.

Breward, Ian.
1972 "The Abolition of Puritanism." *Journal of Religious History* 7: 20-34.

Brewer, Earl D.C.
1952 "Sect and Church in Methodism." *Social Forces* 30: 400-408.

Bridenbaugh, Carl.
1952 *Myths and Realities*. Baton Rouge: Louisiana State.
1962 *Mitre and Sceptre*. New York: Oxford.
1968 *Vexed and Troubled Englishmen*. New York: Oxford.

Brown, Beatrice Curtis.
1968 (ed.). *The Letters and Diplomatic Instructions of Queen Anne*. New York: Funk and Wagnalls [1935].

Brunton, D. and D.H. Pennington.
1954 *Members of the Long Parliament*. London: Allen and Unwin.

Bryant, Arthur.
1968 (ed.). *The Letters, Speeches and Declarations of King Charles II*. New York: Funk and Wagnalls [1935].

Brydon, George MacLaren.
1940 "David Griffith, 1742-1789." *HM* 9: 194-230.
1947 *Virginia's Mother Church and the Political Conditions Under Which it Grew: An Interpretation of the Records of the Colony of Virginia and of the Anglican Church of that Colony, 1607-1727*. Richmond: Virginia Historical Society.
1950 "New Light on the Origins of the Method of Electing Bishops Adopted by the American Episcopal Church." *HM* 19: 202-13.
1952 *Virginia's Mother Church and the Political Conditions Under which it Grew: The Story of the Anglican Church and the Development of Religion in Virginia, 1727-1814*. Philadelphia: Church Historical Society.

Burnyeat, J.P.
1966 "The 'Political' Theology of Thomas Hobbes." *HM* 35: 231-235.

Burr, Nelson R.
1954 *The Anglican Church in New Jersey*. Philadelphia: Church Historical Society.

Bushman, Richard L.
1970 *From Puritan to Yankee*. New York: Norton.

Byrne, M. St. Clare.
1968 (ed.). *The Letters of King Henry VIII*. New York: Funk and Wagnalls [1935].

Cameron, Kenneth Walter.
1970 (ed.). *The Anglican Episcopate in Connecticut*. Hartford: Transcendental.
1972 (ed.). *Letter-Book of the Rev. Henry Caner*. Hartford: Transcendental.

Cantor, Norman F.
1967 *The English*. New York: Simon & Schuster.

Capp, B.S.
1972 *The Fifth Monarchy Men*. Totowa, N.J.: Rowman and Littlefield.

Carroll, Peter N.
1969 *Puritanism and the Wilderness*. New York: Columbia.
1970 (ed.). *Religion and the Coming of the American Revolution*. Waltham, Mass.: Ginn-Blaisdell.

Chamberlayne, John H.
1964 "From Sect to Church in British Methodism." *British Journal of Sociology* 15: 139-149.

Church, R.W.
1970 *The Oxford Movement*. Chicago: Chicago [1891].

Classified Digest.
1893 *Classified Digest of the Records of the Society for the Propagation of the Gospel in Foreign Parts*, 3rd. ed. London: S.P.G.

Clarke, Philip G.
1976 *Anglicanism in South Carolina*. Easley, S.C.: Southern Historical Press.

Cohn, Norman.
1957 *The Pursuit of the Millenium*. Fair Lawn, N.J.: Essential Books.

Coleman, John A.
1968 "Church-Sect Typology and Organizational Precariousness." *SA* 29: 55-66.

Collinson, Patrick.
1967 *The Elizabethan Puritan Movement.* London: Cape.
Coolidge, John.
1970 *The Pauline Renaissance in England.* London: Oxford.
Coser, Lewis A.
1954 "Sects and Sectarians." *Dissent* 1: 360-369.
Cragg, G.R.
1950 *From Puritanism to the Age of Reason.* Cambridge: Cambridge.
1966 "The Collapse of Militant Puritanism." Pp. 76-103 in Bennett and Walsh, 1966.
Cranston, Maurice.
1969 *John Locke.* London: Longmans-Green.
Cremeans, Charles David.
1949 *The Reception of Calvinistic Thought in England.* Urbana: Illinois.
Cross, Arthur Lyon.
1964 *The Anglican Episcopate and the American Colonies.* Hamden, Ct.: Archon [1902].
Cross, Claire.
1969 *The Royal Supremacy in the Elizabethan Church.* London: Allen and Unwin.
1972 "The Church in England, 1646-1660." Pp. 99-120 in Alymer, 1972.
Crowley, Welden S.
1973 "Erastianism in the Westminster Assembly." *JCS* 15: 49-64.
Curteis, George Herbert.
1906 *Dissent in its Relation to the Church of England.* London: Macmillan [1871].
Dalcho, Frederick.
1972 *An Historical Account of the Protestant Episcopal Church in South Carolina.* New York: Arno [1820].
Davidson, Elizabeth H.
1936 *The Establishment of the English Church in the Continental American Colonies.* Durham, N.C.: Duke.
Davidson, Philip.
1973 *Propaganda and the American Revolution, 1763-1783.* New York: Norton [1949].
Davies, Godfrey.
1955 *The Restoration of Charles II, 1658-1660.* San Marino, Ca.: Huntington Library.
Dawley, Powell Mills.
1954 *John Whitgift and the English Reformation.* New York: Scribners.
1961 *The Episcopal Church and its Work,* rev. ed. New York: Seabury.
Demerath, N.J., III.
1967a "In a Sow's Ear." *JSSR* 6: 77-84.
1967b "Son of Sow's Ear." *JSSR* 6: 275-277.
Demerath, N.J., III and Phillip E. Hammond.
1969. *Religion in Social Context.* New York: Random House.
Dickens, A.G.
1964 *The English Reformation.* New York: Schocken.
1967 *Thomas Cromwell and the English Reformation.* London: English Universities.
Dillon, Francis.
1975 *The Pilgrims.* Garden City, N.Y.: Doubleday.
Dittes, James E.
1971 "Typing the Typologies." *JSSR* 10: 375-383.
Dunn, John.
1969 *The Political Thought of John Locke.* Cambridge: Cambridge.

Dynes, Russell R.
1955 "Church-Sect Typology and Socio-Economic Status." *ASR* 20: 555-560.
Eberts, Paul R. and Ronald Witton
1970 "Recall from Anecdote." *ASR* 35: 1081-1097.
Eckenrode, H.J.
1971 *Separation of Church and State in Virginia.* New York: Da Capo [1910].
Eister, Allan W.
1949 "The Oxford Movement." *Sociology and Social Research* 34: 116-24.
1967 "Toward a Radical Critique of Church-Sect Typology." *JSSR* 6: 85-90.
1973 "H. Richard Niebuhr and the Paradox of Religious Organization." Pp. 355-408 in Glock and Hammond, 1973.
Ellis, Joseph.
1973 *The New England Mind in Transition.* New Haven: Yale.
Elton, G.R.
1972 *Policy and Police.* Cambridge: Cambridge.
1973 *Reform and Renewal.* Cambridge: Cambridge.
Fallding, Harold.
1974 *The Sociology of Religion.* Toronto: McGraw-Hill-Ryerson.
Farr, William.
1974 *John Wyclif as Legal Reformer.* Leiden: Brill.
Fenn, Richard K.
1978 *Toward a Theory of Secularization.* Storrs, Ct.: Society for the Scientific Study of Religion.
Ferm, Robert L.
1969 (ed.). *Issues in American Protestantism.* Garden City, N.Y.: Doubleday/Anchor.
Ferré, Frederick.
1969 "Mapping the Logic of Models in Science and Theology." Pp. 54-74 in Dallas M. High (ed.), *New Essays on Religious Language.* New York: Oxford.
Figgis, John Neville.
1914 *The Divine Right of Kings,* 2nd. ed. Cambridge: Cambridge.
Firth, C.H.
1962 *Cromwell's Army.* New York: Barnes & Noble [1900-1901].
Foote, William Henry.
1966 *Sketches of Virginia.* Richmond: John Knox [1850].
Forcese, Dennis P.
1968 "Calvinism, Capitalism and Confusion." *SA* 29: 193-201.
Foster, Elizabeth.
1970 "The Procedure of the House of Commons against Patents and Monopolies, 1621-1624." Pp. 57-85 in Aiken and Henning, 1970.
Foster, John.
1974 *Class Struggle and the Industrial Revolution.* New York: St. Martin's.
Foster, Walter Roland.
1958 *Bishop and Presbytery.* London: S.P.C.K.
Frank, Joseph.
1955 *The Levellers.* Cambridge: Harvard.
Frere, W.H.
1904 *The English Church: In the Reigns of Elizabeth and James I. 1558-1625.* London: Macmillan.
Frere, W.H. and C.E. Douglas.
1954 (eds.). *Puritan Manifestors.* London: S.P.C.K. [1907].

Garrett, Christina Hallowell.
1938 *The Marian Exiles*. Cambridge: Cambridge.
Garrett, William R.
1975 "Maligned Mysticism." *SA* 36: 205-223.
Garrison, Winfred E.
1948 "Characteristics of American Organized Religion." *Annals of the American Academy of Political and Social Science* 256: 14-24.
Gaustad, Edwin Scott.
1957 *The Great Awakening in New England*. New York: Harper and Row.
1968 (ed.). *Religious Issues in American History*. New York: Harper and Row.
1969 "A Disestablished Society." *JCS* 11: 409-25.
Gillin, J.L.
1910 "A Contribution to the Sociology of Sects." *American Journal of Sociology* 16: 236-252.
Glasner, Peter E.
1977 *The Sociology of Secularization*. London: Routledge & Kegan Paul.
Glock, Charles Y. and Phillip E. Hammond.
1973 (eds.). *Beyond the Classics?*. New York: Harper and Row.
Goldie, F.
1951 *A Short History of the Episcopal Church in Scotland*. London: S.P.C.K.
Gooch, G.P.
1954 *English Democratic Ideas in the Seventeenth Century*, 2nd. ed. (H.J. Laski). Cambridge: Cambridge [1927].
Goode, Erich.
1967a "Some Critical Observations on the Church-Sect Dimension." *JSSR* 6: 69-77.
1967b "Further Reflections on the Church-Sect Dimension." *JSSR* 6: 270-275.
Greeley, Andrew M.
1972 *The Denominational Society*. Glenview, Ill.: Scott, Foresman.
Greenleaf, Jonathan.
1846 *History of the Churches in the City of New York*. New York: French.
Gustafson, Paul M.
1967 "UO-US-PS-PO: A Restatement of Troeltsch's Church-Sect Typology." *JSSR* 6: 64-68.
1973 "Exegesis on the Gospel According to St. Max." *SA* 34: 12-25.
1975 "The Missing Member of Troeltsch's Trinity." *SA* 36: 224-226.
Guttridge, G.H.
1966 *English Whiggism and the American Revolution*. Berkeley: California.
Halévy, Elie.
1971. *The Birth of Methodism in England*. Chicago: Chicago [1906].
Hall, David.
1968a (ed.). *The Antinomian Controversy, 1636-1638*. Middletown, Ct.: Wesleyan.
1968b (ed.). *Puritanism in Seventeenth-Century Massachusetts*. New York: Holt, Rinehart, and Winston.
1972 *The Faithful Shepherd*. Williamsburg, Va.: Institute of Early American History and Culture.
Hall, Joseph H., III.
"Joseph Hall, The English Seneca and Champion of Episcopacy." *HM* 21: 62-99.
Haller, William.
1934 (ed.). *Tracts on Liberty in the Puritan Revolution, 1638-1647*. New York: Columbia.

1938 *The Rise of Puritanism*. New York: Columbia.
1955 *Liberty and Reformation in the Puritan Revolution*. New York: Columbia.
1963 *Foxe's Book of Martyrs and the Elect Nation*. London: Cape.
1964 *Elizabeth I and the Puritans*. Ithaca, N.Y.: Cornell.
Haller, William and Godfrey Davies.
1944 (eds.). *The Leveller Tracts, 1647-1653*. New York: Columbia.
Hardacre, Paul H.
1973 "The Genesis of the Declaration of Breda, 1657-1660." *JCS* 15: 65-82.
Harkness, R.E.E.
1933 "Early Relations of Baptists and Quakers." *CH* 2: 227-242.
Harrison, G.B.
1968 (ed.). *The Letters of Queen Elizabeth I*. New York: Funk and Wagnalls [1935].
Hart, A. Tindal.
1968 *Clergy and Society, 1600-1800*. London: S.P.C.K.
Harvey, Richard.
1971 "The Problem of Social-Political Obligation for the Church of England in the Seventeenth Century," *CH* 40: 156-169.
Haugaard, William P.
1968 *Elizabeth and the English Reformation*. Cambridge: Cambridge.
Hawks, Francis L.
1836 *Contributions to the Ecclesiastical History of the United States of America*, vol. I. New York: Harper.
Heberle, Rudolf.
1951 *Social Movements*. New York: Appleton-Century-Crofts.
Heimert, Alan and Perry Miller.
1967 (eds.). *The Great Awakening*. Indianapolis: Bobbs-Merrill.
Herberg, Will.
1954 *Protestant-Catholic-Jew*. Garden City, N.Y.: Doubleday.
1962 "Religion in a Secularized Society." *Review of Religious Research* 3: 145-158; 4: 33-45.
Herklots, H.G.G.
1966 *The Church of England and the American Episcopal Church*. London: Mowbrays.
Hexter, Jack H.
1941 *The Reign of King Pym*. Cambridge: Harvard.
1961 *Reappraisals in History*. London: Longmans.
Hill, [John Edward] Christopher.
1956 *Economic Problems of the Church*. Oxford: Oxford.
1964 *Puritanism and Revolution*. New York: Schocken.
1965 *Intellectual Origins of the English Revolution*. London: Oxford.
1966 *Century of Revolution, 1603-1714*. New York: Norton.
1967 *Society and Puritanism in Pre-Revolutionary England*, 2nd. ed. New York: Schocken.
1969 *Reformation to Industrial Revolution, 1530-1780*. Baltimore: Penguin.
1970 *God's Englishman*. New York: Dial.
1971 *Antichrist in Seventeenth Century England*. London: Oxford.
1972 *The World Turned Upside Down*. London: Temple Smith.
1975 *Change and Continuity in Seventeenth-Century England*. Cambridge: Harvard.
1978 *Milton and the English Revolution*. New York: Viking.

Hill, Michael.
1973 "They Changed Our Thinking: VI. Max Weber (1864-1920)." *Expository Times* 84: 260-265.

Hillerbrand, Hans J.
1964 (ed.). *The Reformation.* New York: Harper and Row.

Hood, Fred J.
1971 "Revolution and Religious Liberty." *CH* 40: 170-181.

Hooker, Richard.
1907 *Of the Laws of Ecclesiastical Polity.* London: Dent [1594].

Howard, K.W.H.
1975 (ed.). *The Axminster Ecclesiastica, 1660-1698.* Sheffield: Gospel Tidings.

Howell, Roger, Jr.
1977 *Cromwell.* Boston: Little-Brown.

Hudson, Winthrop S.
1955 "Denominationalism as a Basis for Ecumenicity." *CH* 24: 32-50.

Hutchinson, F.E.
1962 *Cranmer and the English Reformation.* New York: Collier.

Hutton, William Holden.
1913 *The English Church: From the Accession of Charles I to the Death of Anne, 1625-1714.* London: Macmillan.

Isichei, Elizabeth Allo.
1964 "From Sect to Denomination in English Quakerism." *British Journal of Sociology* 15: 207-222.

Israel, Herman.
1966 "Some Religious Factors in the Emergence of Industrial Society in England." *ASR* 31: 589-599.

James, F.G.
1970 "The Bishops in Politics, 1688-1714." Pp. 227-257 in Aiken and Henning, 1970.

James, Margaret.
1966 ·*Social Problems and Policy during the Puritan Revolution.* New York: Barnes and Noble.

James, Walter.
1962 *The Christian in Politics.* London: Oxford.

Jessett, Thomas E.
1952 "Planting the Prayer Book in Puritan Massachusetts." *HM* 21: 299-406.

Johnson, Benton.
1957 "A Critical Appraisal of Church-Sect Typology." *ASR* 22: 88-92.
1963 "On Church and Sect." *ASR* 28: 539-49.
1971 "Church and Sect Revisited." *JSSR* 10: 124-137.

Jones, J.R.
1972 *The Revolution of 1688 in England.* New York: Norton.

Jones, James W.
1973 *The Shattered Synthesis.* New Haven: Yale.

Jones, W.J.
1971 *Politics and the Bench.* New York: Barnes and Noble.

Jordan, W.K.
1942 *Men of Substance.* Chicago: Chicago.
1965 *The Development of Religious Toleration in England.* Gloucester, Mass.: Smith [4 vols.: 1932-1940].

Kelly, J. Thomas.
1977 *Thorns on the Tudor Rose.* Jackson: University Press of Mississippi.

Kenyon, J.P.
1966 (ed.). *The Stuart Constitution.* Cambridge: Cambridge.

Klingberg, Arthur J.
1940 ·*Anglican Humanitarianism in Colonial New York.* Philadelphia: Church Historical Society.

Knappen, Marshall M.
1970 *Tudor Puritanism.* Chicago: Chicago.

Knudsen, Dean D., John R. Earle, and Donald W. Shriver, Jr.
1978 "The Conception of Sectarian Religion." *Review of Religious Research* 20: 44-60.

Lacey, Douglas R.
1969 *Dissent and Parliamentary Politics in England, 1661-1689.* New Brunswick, N.J.: Rutgers.

Lamont, William M.
1963 *Marginal Prynne, 1600-1669.* London: Routledge and Kegan Paul.
1969 *Godly Rule.* London: Macmillan.

Leatherbarrow, J. Stanley.
1947 *The Lancashire Elizabethan Recusants.* Manchester: Chetham Society.

Legg, L.G. Wickham.
1964 "The Coronation Service," Pp. 690-702 in W.K. Lowther Clarke (ed.), *Liturgy and Worship.* London: S.P.C.K. [1932].

Lehmberg, Stanford E.
1970 *The Reformation Parliament, 1529-1536.* Cambridge: Cambridge.

Leites, Edmund.
1978 "Conscience, Leisure, and Learning." *SA* 39: 36-61.

Lindsay, A.D.
1962 *The Modern Democratic State.* New York: Oxford [1943].

Lipset, Seymour Martin.
1964 "Religion and Politics in the American Past and Present." Pp. 69-126 in Robert Lee and Martin E. Marty (eds.), *Religion and Social Conflict.* New York: Oxford.
1967 *The First New Nation.* Garden City, N.Y.: Doubleday/Anchor.

Littell, Franklin Hamlin.
1962 *From State Church to Pluralism.* Garden City, N.Y.: Doubleday/Anchor.
1969 *The Church and the Body Politic.* New York: Seabury.

Little, David.
1969 *Religion, Order, and Law.* New York: Harper and Row.
1974a "Max Weber and the Comparative Study of Religious Ethics." *Journal of Religious Ethics* 2: 5-40.
1974b "The Origins of Perplexity." Pp. 185-210 in Russell E. Richey and Donald G. Jones (eds.), *American Civil Religion.* New York: Harper and Row.
1976 "Religion, Morality, and the State." Paper presented at the annual meeting of the Society for the Scientific Study of Religion. Philadelphia.

Liu, Tai.
1973 *Discord in Zion.* The Hague: Nijhoff.

Lovejoy, David S.
1972 *The Glorious Revolution in America.* New York: Harper and Row.

Loveland, Clara O.
1956 *The Critical Years.* Greenwich, Ct.: Seabury.

Lucas, Stephen E.
1976 *Portents of Rebellion.* Philadelphia: Temple.

Luckmann, Thomas.
1967 *The Invisible Religion.* New York: Macmillan.

McAdoo, Henry R.
　1965　*The Spirit of Anglicanism*. New York: Scribners.
Macaulay, Thomas Babington.
　1967　*History of England*. London: Heron [4 vols.: 1848-1861].
MacDonald, William W.
　1973　"Anticlericalism, Protestantism, and the English Reformation." *JCS* 15: 21-32.
McGiffert, Michael.
　1969　(ed.). *Puritanism and the American Experience*. Reading, Ma.: Addison-Wesley.
McGinn, Donald Joseph.
　1949　*The Admonition Controversy*. New Brunswick, N.J.: Rutgers.
McGrath, Patrick.
　1967　*Papists and Puritans under Elizabeth I*. New York: Walker.
McKinney, John C.
　1966　*Constructive Typology and Social Theory*. New York: Appleton-Century-Crofts.
McLoughlin William G.
　1971　*New England Dissent, 1630-1833*. Cambridge: Harvard.
MacPherson, C.B.
　1962　*The Political Theory of Possessive Individualism*. Oxford: Oxford.
Maier, Pauline.
　1974　*From Resistance to Revolution*. New York: Random House/Vintage.
Manning, Bernard Lord.
　1952　*The Protestant Dissenting Deputies*. Cambridge: Cambridge.
　1967　*The Making of Modern English Religion*. London: Independent [1929].
Manning, Roger Burrow.
　1969　*Religion and Society in Elizabethan Sussex*. Leicester: Leicester.
Manross, William Wilson.
　1938　*The Episcopal Church in the United States, 1800-1840*. New York: Columbia.
　1959　*A History of the American Episcopal Church*, rev. ed. New York: Morehouse.
Marsden, George, M.
　1970　"Perry Miller's Rehabilitation of the Puritans." *CH* 39: 91-105.
Marshall, John S.
　1948　(ed.). *Hooker's Polity in Modern English*. Sewanee, Tn.: University [of the South].
Martin, David.
　1962　"The Denomination." *British Journal of Sociology* 13: 1-14.
　1966　*Pacifism*. New York: Schocken.
　1967　*A Sociology of English Religion*. New York: Basic Books.
　1969　*The Religious and the Secular*. New York: Schocken.
　1978　*A General Theory of Secularization*. New York: Barnes & Noble.
Marty, Martin E.
　1969　*The Modern Schism*. New York: Harper and Row.
　1970　*Righteous Empire*. New York: Dial.
　1976　"Living with Establishment and Disestablishment in Nineteenth-Century Anglo-America." *JCS* 18: 61-77.
Mason, A.J.
　1913　*The Church of England and Episcopacy*. Cambridge: Cambridge.
Mayrl, William W.
　1976　"'Marx' Theory of Social Movements and the Church-Sect Typology." *SA* 37: 19-31.

Mead, Sidney E.
　1963　*The Lively Experiment*. New York: Harper and Row.
　1971　"The Fact of Pluralism and the Persistence of Sectarianism." Pp. 247-266 in E.A. Smith, 1971.
　1975　*The Nation with the Soul of a Church*. New York: Harper and Row.
Merton, Robert K.
　1970　*Science, Technology and Society in Seventeenth Century England*. New York: Harper and Row [1938].
Meza, Pedro Thomas.
　1973　"The Question of Authority in the Church of England, 1689-1717." *HM* 42: 63-86.
Middlekauf, Robert.
　1971　*The Mathers*. New York: Oxford.
Midwinter, Edward.
　1933　"The S.P.G. and the Colonial Church in Massachusetts." *HM* 4: 100-115.
Miller, Perry.
　1935　"The Contribution of the Protestant Churches to Religious Liberty in Colonial America." *CH* 4: 57-66.
　1956a　(ed.). *The American Puritans*. Garden City, N.Y.: Doubleday/Anchor.
　1956b　*Errand into the Wilderness*. New York: Harper and Row.
　1961a　*The New England Mind: The Seventeenth Century*. Boston: Beacon [1939].
　1961b　*The New England Mind: From Colony to Province*. Boston: Beacon [1953].
　1965　*The Life of the Mind in America, from the Revolution to the Civil War*. New York: Harcourt, Brace, and World.
　1970　*Orthodoxy in Massachusetts* (intro. David D. Hall). New York: Harper and Row [1933].
Miller, Perry and Thomas H. Johnson.
　1963　(eds.). *The Puritans* (rev. George McCandlish). New York: Harper and Row.
Mills, Frederick V., Sr.
　1978　*Bishops by Ballot*. New York: Oxford.
Mitchell, Williams M.
　1957　*The Rise of the Revolutionary Party in the English House of Commons*. New York: Columbia.
Moberg, David O.
　1961　"Potential Uses of the Church-Sect Typology in Comparative Religious Research." *International Journal of Comparative Sociology* 2: 47-58.
Mol, J.J.
　1968　*The Breaking of Traditions*. Berkeley: Glendessary.
Moorman, John R.H.
　1963　*A History of the Church in England*, rev. ed. London: Black.
More, Paul Elmer and Frank Leslie Cross.
　1951　*Anglicanism*. London: S.P.C.K. [1935].
Morehouse, Clifford P.
　1973　*Trinity*. New York: Seabury.
Morgan, Edmund Sears.
　1956　*The Birth of the Republic, 1763-1789*. Chicago: Chicago.
　1958　*The Puritan Dilemma*. Boston: Little-Brown.
　1959　(ed.). *Prologue to Revolution*. Williamsburg, Va.: Institute of Early American History and Culture.
　1963　*Visible Saints*. New York: N.Y.U.
Mosca, Gaetano.
　1935　"Church, Sects and Parties." *Social Forces* 14: 53-63.

105

Mott, Royden J.
   1934 "Sources of Jefferson's Ecclesiastical Views." *CH* 3: 267-284.
Mueller, Gert H.
   1973 "Asceticism and Mysticism." *International Yearbook for the Sociology of Religion* 8: 68-132.
   1977 "The Notion of Rationality in the Work of Max Weber." Paper presented at the University of Wisconsin-Milwaukee Colloquia and Symposia on Max Weber: mimeographed.
Munz, Peter.
   1952 *The Place of Hooker in the History of Thought.* London: Routledge and Kegan Paul.
Neale, J.E.
   [1952] *Elizabeth I and her Parliaments, 1559-1581.* New York: British Book Centre.
Neill, Stephen.
   1965 *Anglicanism,* 3rd. ed. Baltimore: Penguin.
Nelson, Benjamin.
   1973 "Weber's Protestant Ethic." Pp. 71-130 in Glock and Hammond, 1973.
   1974 "Max Weber's 'Author's Introduction' (1920)." *Sociological Inquiry* 44: 269-278.
   1975 "Max Weber, Ernst Troeltsch, Georg Jellinek as Comparative Historical Sociologists." *SA* 36: 229-240.
   1976 "On Orient and Occident in Max Weber." *Social Research* 43: 114-129.
Nelson, William.
   1909 *The Controversy over the Proposition for an American Episcopate, 1767-1774: A Bibliography of the Subject.* Paterson, N.J.: Paterson History Club.
New, J.F.H.
   1964 *Anglican and Puritan.* Palo Alto, Ca.: Stanford.
Niebuhr, H. Richard.
   1929 *The Social Sources of Denominationalism.* New York: Holt.
Niebuhr, Reinhold and Alan Heimert.
   1963 *A Nation So Conceived.* New York: Scribners.
Nuttall, Geoffrey F.
   1957 *Visible Saints.* Oxford: Blackwell.
O'Connell, Marvin R.
   1969 *The Oxford Conspirators.* New York: Macmillan.
O'Dea, Thomas.
   1968 "Sects and Cults." *International Encyclopedia of the Social Sciences.* New York: Macmillan.
Olsen, V. Norskov.
   1973 *John Foxe and the Elizabethan Church.* Berkeley: California.
Orr, Robert R.
   1967 *Reason and Authority.* London: Oxford.
O'Toole, Roger.
   1975 "Sectarianism in Politics." Pp. 162-189 in Wallis, 1975b.
   1976 " 'Underground' Traditions in the Study of Sectarianism." *JSSR* 15: 145-156.
Ozment, Steven E.
   1973 *Mysticism and Dissent.* New Haven: Yale.
Park, Robert E.
   1967 "Characteristics of the Sect." Pp. 240-248 in Ralph H. Turner (ed.). *On Social Control and Collective Behavior.* Chicago: Chicago [1932].

Parker, T.M.
   1966 *The English Reformation to 1558,* 2nd. ed. London: Oxford.
Parsons, Edward Lambe and Bayard Hale Jones.
   1937 *The American Prayer Book.* New York: Scribners.
Parsons, Talcott.
   1964 "Christianity and Modern Industrial Society." Pp. 273-298 in Louis Schneider (ed.), *Religion, Culture and Society.* New York: Wiley.
Pearson, Samuel C., Jr.
   1969 "Reluctant Radicals." *JCS* 11: 473-486.
Peck, William George.
   1933 *The Social Implications of the Oxford Movement.* New York: Scribners.
Pennington, Edgar L.
   1954 *The Church of England and the Reformation.* Eton: Savile.
Pepper, George B.
   1963 "A Re-examination of the Ideal Type Concept." *SA* 24: 185-201.
Perry, Ralph Barton.
   1944 *Puritanism and Democracy.* New York: Vanguard.
Petegorsky, David W.
   1940 *Left-Wing Democracy in the English Civil War.* London: Gollancz.
Pfautz, Harold W.
   1955 "The Sociology of Secularization." *American Journal of Sociology* 61: 121-128.
Pilcher, George William.
   1971 *Samuel Davies.* Knoxville: Tennessee.
Plummer, Alfred.
   1904 *English Church History.* Edinburgh: Clarke.
Polishook, Irwin H.
   1967 (ed.). *Roger Williams, John Cotton and Religious Freedom.* Englewood Cliffs, N.J.: Prentice-Hall.
Pollard, A.F.
   1929 *Wolsey.* London: Longmans.
   1966 *Henry VIII.* New York: Harper and Row [1902].
Pope, Robert G.
   1969 *The Half-Way Covenant.* Princeton: Princeton.
Powicke, Frederick M.
   1942 *The Reformation in England.* London: Oxford.
Proctor, Francis and Walter Howard Frere.
   1965 *A New History of the Book of Common Prayer,* 3rd. ed. London: Macmillan [1905].
Pulman, Michael Barraclough.
   1971 *The Elizabethan Privy Council in the Fifteen-Seventies.* Berkeley: California.
Rainbolt, John Corbin.
   1975 "The Struggle to Define 'Religious Liberty' in Maryland, 1776-85." *JCS* 17: 443-458.
Redekop, Calvin.
   1974 "A New Look at Sect Development." *JSSR* 13: 345-352.
Reist, Benjamin.
   1967 *Toward a Theology of Involvement.* Philadelphia: Westminster.
Rice, Hugh A. Lawrence.
   1961 *The Bridge Builders.* New York: Longmans.
Richardson, Caroline Francis.
   1928 *English Preachers and Preaching, 1640-1670.* London: S.P.C.K.

Ritcheson, Charles R.
1954 *British Politics and the American Revolution.* Norman: Oklahoma.
Robbins, Caroline.
1959 *The Eighteenth Century Commonwealthman.* Cambridge: Harvard.
Robertson, D.B.
1951 *The Religious Foundations of Leveller Democracy.* New York: King's Crown.
Robertson, Roland.
1970 *The Sociological Interpretation of Religion.* New York: Schocken.
1975 "On the Analysis of Mysticism." *SA* 36: 241-266.
1977 "Church-Sect and Rationality." *JSSR* 16: 197-200.
1978 *Meaning and Change.* New York: N.Y.U.
Rodes, R.E.
1969 "The Last Days of Erastianism." *Harvard Theological Review* 62: 301-348.
Rodgers, George C.
1959 *Church and State in Eighteenth-Century South Carolina.* Charleston: Dalcho Historical Society.
Rogers, Rolf E.
1969 *Max Weber's Ideal Type Theory.* New York: Philosophical Library.
Roots, Ivan.
1966 *The Great Rebellion, 1642-1660.* London: Batsford.
Rossiter, Clinton.
1956 *The First American Revolution.* New York: Harcourt, Brace and World.
Rowse, A.L.
1950 *The England of Elizabeth.* New York: Harper and Row.
1959 *The Elizabethans and America.* New York: Harper and Row.
1965 *The Expansion of Elizabethan England.* New York: Harper and Row [1955].
Salomon, Richard G.
1951 "British Legislation and American Episcopacy." *HM* 20: 278-293.
Scalf, John H., Michael J. Miller, and Charles W. Thomas.
1973 "Goal Specificity, Organizational Structure, and Participant Commitment in Churches." *SA* 34: 169-184.
Schenk, W.
1948 *The Concern for Social Justice in the Puritan Revolution.* London: Longmans.
Schlatter, Richard B.
1971 *The Social Ideas of Religious Leaders, 1660-1688.* New York: Farrar, Straus, and Giroux.
Schneider, Herbert W. and Carol Schneider.
1929 *Samuel Johnson, President of King's College,* vol. III. New York: Columbia.
Schwartz, Gary.
1970 *Sect Ideologies and Social Status.* Chicago: Chicago.
Searle, Clayton Stanley.
1969 "William Laud and the System of 'Thorough'." Unpublished PhD. dissertation. New York: Columbia University.
Seaver, Paul S.
1970 *The Puritan Lectureships.* Palo Alto, Ca.: Stanford.
Selbie, W.B.
[1912] *Nonconformity.* London: Williams and Norgate.
Seymour, Urigen Storrs.
1933 *The Beginnings of the Episcopal Church in Connecticut.* New Haven: Yale.

Shiner, Larry.
1967 "The Concept of Secularization in Empirical Research." *JSSR* 6: 207-220.
Shirley, F.J.
1949 *Richard Hooker and Contemporary Political Ideas.* London: S.P.C.K.
Shoemaker, Robert W.
1959 *The Origin and Meaning of the Name "Protestant Episcopal".* New York: American Church.
Simpson, Alan.
1955 *Puritanism in Old and New England.* Chicago: Chicago.
1961 *The Wealth of the Gentry, 1540-1660.* Cambridge: Cambridge.
Smelser, Neil.
1963 *The Theory of Collective Behavior.* New York: Free Press.
Smith, Elwyn A.
1971 (ed.). *The Religion of the Republic.* Philadelphia: Fortress.
1972 *Religious Liberty in the United States.* Philadelphia: Fortress.
Smith, Lacey Baldwin.
1953 *Tudor Prelates and Politics, 1536-1558.* Princeton: Princeton.
Smith, Page
1976 (ed.).*Religious Origins of the American Revolution.* Missoula, Mt.: Scholars.
Smylie, James H.
1971 "Protestant Clergy, the First Amendment and Beginnings of a Constitutional Debate, 1781-91." Pp. 116-153 in E.A. Smith, 1971.
Snapp, Harry F.
1973 "Church and State Relations in Early Eighteenth-Century England." *JCS* 15: 83-96.
Snook, John B.
1974 "An Alternative to Church-Sect." *JSSR* 13: 191-204.
Soloway, Richard Allen.
1969 *Prelates and People.* London: Routledge and Kegan Paul.
Spalding, James C.
1976 "Restitutionism as a Normative Factor for Puritan Dissent." *Journal of the American Academy of Religion* 44: 47-63.
Sperry, Willard L.
1946 *Religion in America.* New York: Macmillan.
Stearns, R.P.
1940 *Congregationalism in the Dutch Netherlands.* Chicago: American Society of Church History.
Steeman, Theodore M.
1975 "Church, Sect, Mysticism, Denomination." *SA* 36: 181-204.
Steiner, Bruce E.
1971 *Samuel Seabury, 1729-1796.* Athens: Ohio.
Stith, William.
1865 *The History of the First Discovery and Settlement of Virginia.* New York: Reprinted for Joseph Sabin [1747].
Stone, Lawrence.
1961 *The Crisis of Aristocracy, 1558-1641.* London: Oxford.
1972 *The Causes of the English Revolution, 1529-1642.* New York: Harper and Row.
Straka, Gerald M.
1962 *Anglican Reaction to the Revolution of 1688.* Madison: State Historical Society of Wisconsin.

Strickland, R.C.
1939 *Religion and the State in Georgia in the Eighteenth Century.* New York: Columbia.

Sweet, William Warren.
1935 "The American Colonial Environment and Religious Liberty." *CH* 4: 43-56.
1965 *Religion in Colonial America.* New York: Cooper Square [1942].

Switzer, Gerald B.
1932 "The Suppression of Convocation in the Church of England." *CH* 1: 150-162.

Sykes, Norman.
1934 *Church and State in England in the Eighteenth Century.* Cambridge: Cambridge.
1956 *Old Priest and New Presbyter.* Cambridge: Cambridge.

Tanner, J.R.
1928 *English Constitutional Conflicts of the Seventeenth Century.* Cambridge: Cambridge.

Tawney, R.H.
1960 *Religion and the Rise of Capitalism.* New York: New American Library [1922].

Temple, Sydney A., Jr.
1946 *The Common Sense Theology of Bishop White.* New York: King's Crown.

Thomas, Keith.
1965 "The Social Origins of Hobbes' Political Thought." Pp. 185-236 in K.C. Brown (ed.), *Hobbes Studies.* Oxford: Blackwell.
1972 "The Levellers and the Franchise." Pp. 57-78 in Alymer, 1972.

Thompson, E.P.
1963 *The Making of the English Working Class.* New York: Random House.

Thompson, Kenneth A.
1970 *Bureaucracy and Church Reform.* London: Oxford.

Thoms, Herbert.
1963 *Samuel Seabury.* Hamden, Ct.: Shoe String.

Tiffany, Charles C.
1907 *A History of the Protestant Episcopal Church in the United States of America,* 3rd ed. New York: Scribners.

Tolmie, Murray.
1977 *The Triumph of the Saints.* Cambridge: Cambridge.

Toon, Peter.
1970 (ed.). *Puritans, the Millenium, and the Future of Israel.* Cambridge: Clarke.

Trevelyan, George Macaulay.
1954 *England under the Stuarts.* London: Methuen [1904].

Trevor-Roper, Hugh R.
1962 *Archbishop Laud, 1573-1645,* 2nd. ed. Hamden, Ct.: Archon.
1972 *Religion, the Reformation and Social Change,* 2nd. ed. London: Macmillan.

Trinterud, Leonard J.
1951 "The Origins of Puritanism." *CH* 20: 37-57.
1971 (ed.). *Elizabethan Puritanism.* New York: Oxford.

Troeltsch, Ernst.
1931 *The Social Teachings of the Christian Church,* vol. I. New York: Macmillan.

Tyng, Dudley.
1960 *Massachusetts Episcopalians, 1607-1957.* Pascoag, R.I.: Delmo.

Underdown, David.
1960 *Royalist Conspiracy in England, 1649-1660.* New Haven: Yale.
1971 *Pride's Purge.* Oxford: Oxford.

Usher, Roland G.
1910 *The Reconstruction of the English Church.* New York: Appleton.
1913 *The Rise and Fall of the High Commission.* Oxford: Oxford.
1918 *The Pilgrims and. their History.* New York: Macmillan.

VanderMolen, Ronald J.
1973 "Anglican against Puritan." *CH* 42: 45-57.

Vaughn, Alden T.
1972 (ed.). *The Puritan Tradition in America.* Columbia: South Carolina.

Voegelin, Eric.
1952 *The New Science of Politics.* Chicago: Chicago.

Wakeman, Henry Offley.
1887 *The Church and the Puritans.* London: Longmans.

Walker, D.P.
1964 *The Decline of Hell.* London: Routledge & Kegan Paul.

Wallerstein, Immanuel.
1974 *The Modern World-System.* New York: Academic Press.

Wallis, Roy.
1975a "Scientology." *Sociology* 9: 89-100.
1975b (ed.). *Sectarianism.* London: Owen.

Walzer, Michael.
1966 *The Revolution of the Saints.* London: Weidenfeld and Nicolson.

Warch, Richard.
1973 *School of the Prophets.* New Haven: Yale.

Warrender, Howard.
1957 *The Political Philosophy of Hobbes.* Oxford: Oxford.

Watson, D.R.
1972 *The Life and Times of Charles I.* London: Weidenfeld and Nicolson.

Watts, Michael R.
1978 *The Dissenters.* Oxford: Oxford.

Weber, Max.
1930 *The Protestant Ethic and the Spirit of Capitalism.* New York: Scribners.
1947 *The Theory of Social and Economic Organization.* New York: Free Press.
1949 *The Methodology of the Social Sciences.* New York: Free Press.
1950 *General Economic History.* Glencoe, Ill.: Free Press.
1958 *From Max Weber.* New York: Oxford.
1963 *The Sociology of Religion.* Boston: Beacon.
1968 *Economy and Society.* New York: Bedminster.
1973 "Max Weber on Church, Sect, and Mysticism." *SA* 34: 140-149.

Wedgwood, C.V.
1964 *The Trial of Charles I.* London: Collins.

Welch, Michael R.
1977 "Analyzing Religious Sects." *JSSR* 16: 125-139.

Westfall, Richard S.
1970 *Science and Religion in Seventeenth-Century England.* Hamden, Ct.: Archon.

White, William.
1880 *Memoirs of the Protestant Episcopal Church in the United States* (intro. B.F. DeCosta). New York: Dutton [1820].
1954 *The Case of the Protestant Episcopal Churches in the United States Considered.* Philadelphia: Church Historical Society [1782].

Williams, Ethyn M.
1930 "Erastianism in the Great Rebellion." *Church Quarterly Review* 110: 23-33.

Willison, George F.
1964 *Saints and Strangers.* New York: Time [1945].
Wills, Garry.
1978 *Inventing America.* Garden City, N.Y.: Doubleday.
Wilson, Bryan R.
1959 "An Analysis of Sect Development." *ASR* 24: 3-15.
1961 *Sects and Society.* London: Heinemann.
1963 "Typologie des sectes dans une perspective dynamique et comparative." *Archives de Sociologie des Religions* 16: 49-63.
1966 *Religion in Secular Society.* London: Watts.
1967 (ed.). *Patterns of Sectarianism.* London: Heinemann.
1969 "A Typology of Sects." Pp. 361-383 in Roland Robertson (ed.), *Sociology of Religion.* Baltimore: Penguin.
1971 *Religious Sects.* London: Weidenfeld and Nicolson.
1973 *Magic and the Millennium.* New York: Harper and Row.
1979 "The Return of the Sacred." *JSSR* 18: 268-280.
Wilson, H.A.
1912 *Episcopacy and Unity.* London: Longmans.
Wilson, John F.
1965 (ed.). *Church and State in American History.* Boston: Heath.
1969 *Pulpit in Parliament.* Princeton: Princeton.
Winch, Peter.
1958 *The Idea of a Social Science.* London: Routledge and Kegan Paul.
Winton, Ruth M.
1948 "Governor Francis Nicholson's Relations with the Society for the Propagation of the Gospel in Foreign Parts, 1701-1727." *HM* 17: 274-286.

Woodhouse, A.S.P.
1974 (ed.). *Puritanism and Liberty,* 2nd. ed. Chicago: Chicago [1951].
Woodruff, Clinton Rogers.
1944 "The Part of Dr. Routh in Dr. Seabury's Consecration." *HM* 9: 231-246.
Worden, Blair.
1974 *The Rump Parliament, 1648-1653.* New York: Cambridge.
Wright, Louis B.
1962 *The Cultural Life of the American Colonies, 1607-1763.* New York: Harper and Row.
Wuthnow, Robert.
1976 "Recent Patterns of Secularization." *ASR* 41: 850-867.
Yinger, J. Milton.
1946 *Religion and the Struggle for Power.* Durham, N.C.: Duke.
1948 "The Sociology of Religion of Ernst Troeltsch." Pp. 309-315 in Harry Elmer Barnes (ed.), *An Introduction to the History of Sociology.* Chicago: Chicago.
1957 *Religion, Society and the Individual.* New York: Macmillan.
1970 *The Scientific Study of Religion.* New York: Macmillan.
Yule, George.
1958 *The Independents in the English Civil War.* Cambridge: Cambridge.
1968 "Independents and Revolutionaries." *Journal of British Studies* 7: 11-32.
Zagorin, Perez.
1954 *A History of Political Thought in the English Revolution.* London: Routledge and Kegan Paul.
1970 *The Court and the Country.* New York: Atheneum.
Ziff, Larzer.
1973 *Puritanism in America.* New York: Viking.

AUTHOR INDEX

SUBJECT INDEX

0748